"Since his screenplay for D. H. Lawrence's *Women in Love* in 1969, Larry Kramer has been a prophet of psychic health and catastrophe among us— a prophet unmatched for the accuracy of his omens and the reliability of his anathemas and remedies. His uncannily foresighted novel *Faggots* appeared in 1978 just as the AIDS virus flooded whole wings of the American bloodstream; now its Swiftian portrait of an all but vanished subculture stands as that culture's visible memorial. His later plays have been clear as firebells, memorable as tracer bullets."—The American Academy of Arts and Letters citation, May 1996

Praise for *The Normal Heart*

"The blood that's coursing through *The Normal Heart* is boiling hot. There can be little doubt that it is the most outspoken play around."—Frank Rich, *The New York Times*

"Kramer's astounding drama about AIDS is too urgent to ignore! An astounding drama . . . a damning indictment of a nation in the middle of an epidemic with its head in the sand. It will make your hair stand on end even as the tears spurt from your eyes. Dynamite!"—Liz Smith, *New York Daily News*

"Wired with anger, electric with rage . . . Powerful stuff."—*The Boston Globe*

"No one who cares about the future of the human race can afford to miss *The Normal Heart*."—Rex Reed

"*The Normal Heart* has broken a great silence. . . . It has put politics and journalism to shame for the cover-up of a major disaster and one of the great moral dramas of our time."—Frances FitzGerald, author of *Fire in the Lake*

"Impassioned writing . . . explosively powerful . . . uniquely important." —*The Advocate*

"I haven't been this involved—*upset*—in too damn long. Kramer honors us with this stormy, articulate theatrical work."—Harold Prince

"Larry Kramer's *The Normal Heart* is arguably the best political play of that schizophrenic decade and definitely the definitive dramatic exploration of the early years of the AIDS crisis."—*Chicago Tribune*

"Larry Kramer's 1988 masterwork refuses to date."—*Chicago Reader*

"Kramer's play actually may work better now in the tragic hindsight of history."—*Chicago Sun-Times.*

Praise for *The Destiny of Me*

"Searing!"—*Vanity Fair*

"Gives new hope to the American theater. One of the year's ten best . . . Poignant, most moving, enriching."—*Time*

"Overwhelmingly powerful . . . scaldingly honest . . . a seismic jolt of visceral theatricality!"—Frank Rich, *The New York Times*

"A harrowing, emotionally naked family-memory-AIDS play, playful and moving, personable and disturbing, with scenes of devastating counterpoint. The work of a theater artist . . . like Arthur Miller at his best."—*Newsday*

"Driven by a fierce honesty and searing pain, Kramer's emotional and moral urgency fills *The Destiny of Me* with irresistible human truth."—*Newsweek*

"A mature work by a gifted American playwright in his prime . . . bitter and angry and full of biting humor."—*The Wall Street Journal*

"*The Destiny of Me* is bigger than any one of us. The *Long Day's Journey* comparisons are apt. At long last Kramer the activist has leashed in Kramer the polemicist, letting loose Kramer the artist."—*QW*

"*The Destiny of Me* is a beautiful, somber play, very mature, and very personal. Plays are meant for presentation. Great plays also stand well as great literature. This is one of them. Kramer proves once again his place as one of the best writers of our times."—*Lambda Book Report*

The Normal Heart

and

The Destiny of Me

By Larry Kramer

Fiction
Faggots

Plays
Sissies' Scrapbook
The Normal Heart
Just Say No
The Destiny of Me

Screenplay
Women in Love

Nonfiction
Reports from the holocaust: the story of an AIDS activist

The Normal Heart

and

The Destiny of Me

Two plays by Larry Kramer

With a Foreword by Tony Kushner

Grove Press
New York

Library of Congress Cataloging-in-Publication Data

Kramer, Larry.
    The normal heart ; and, The destiny of me / Larry Kramer.
        p. cm.
            ISBN-13: 978-0-8021-3692-3
        1. AIDS (Disease)—Patients—Drama. 2. Gay men—Drama. I. Title: Normal heart; and, The destiny of me. II. Kramer, Larry. Destiny of me. III. Title: Destiny of me. IV. Title.

PS3561.R252 N6 2000
812'.54—dc21   00-024177

Grove Press
an imprint of Grove/Atlantic, Inc.
154 West 14th Street
New York, NY 10011
Distributed by Publishers Group West
www.groveatlantic.com

14 15 16 17 18   10 9 8 7 6

Foreword

1.

Here are two plays that, taken together, offer a persuasive account of a critical, terrible era when an emergent community, laboring to set itself free from centuries of persecution and oppression, was blindsided just at the moment of a political and cultural attainment of some of its most important goals by a biological horror miserably allied to the world's murderous indifference, its masked and its naked hatred. From the time of their first theatrical productions, every concerned, engaged person has had to address, to laud or deplore, to argue and contend with, Larry Kramer's portrayal of the period. The plays are now part of our history, beyond forgetting.

Kramer, not understanding that theater had ceased to be newsworthy, wrote a play that made news, made a difference, had an effect—not to win prizes or encomia in the press, nor to set the box office ablaze, but to catalyze his society, which we all know theater can't do anymore, except on the rare occasions when it does, as when Larry Kramer wrote *The Normal Heart*.

The Normal Heart and *The Destiny of Me* need no introduction because they are accessible to any reader. You don't need permission; don't even knock, just *enter*. You will know immediately that you have been awaited impatiently; you will know immediately where you are and how to proceed. Guides aren't necessary. The plays are shockingly, uncomfortably, almost embarrassingly direct. They contain hidden depths and complexities, to be sure, but in both plays beats one great heart aflame with one grand overwhelming desire: to use dramatic literature and the stage to get at truth, at *a* truth, at one truth of these times—and not a metaphysical truth, not an abstracted principle of existence (though these are, in the process, uncovered), but rather truth as Marx understood it, truth that springs from and returns to action, truth engaged with practice, *praxis*, truth that is shaped by and shapes lived experience, truth that is changed by and changes the world.

The ardency of Kramer's longing for truth is most evident in the language he employs, which is startlingly plain. Although the plays' titles are found in lines of verse by two great poets, W. H. Auden and Walt Whitman, these dramas are remarkably non-poetical, almost antipoetical. Each text has precisely one, and only one symbolic, metaphoric moment which gains much of its power from its absolute isolation. Both moments—the spilled milk in *The Normal Heart*, the spilled blood in *The Destiny of Me*—are actions, stage images; neither is a figure of speech, of language. The writing avoids metaphor, avoids all painterliness. It is governed by a stark, unyielding economy, pressed by a urgent need to find answers and understanding—as pressed by need as the playwright, his protagonist, and the community to which they belong, for which they feel such love and such anger, are pressed to find a cure for AIDS.

The poem that concludes the English-language edition of Bertolt Brecht's *Collected Poems*, "And I Always Thought," could serve as a credo for Kramer's playwriting:

> And I always thought: the very simplest words
> Must be enough. When I say what things are like
> Everyone's heart must be torn to shreds.

That you'll go down if you don't stand up for yourself
Surely you see that.

As in Kramer, so too in much of Brecht: the few instances of metaphor in the writing ring like perfectly cast bells (usually of alarm), precisely because of their scarcity. The ear of the listener, having been opened by the playwright to the logic and rhythms of exigent, functional speech, the speech of crisis, emergency, danger, receives metaphor as an exceptional occurrence, avidly, with heightened attention. This is the way classical writers, the best Greeks and Romans, Aeschylus and Horace, use metaphor: sparingly, with severe discipline. It is a canny technique, but it is much more than a technique. This precision and harshness is the soul of an art that seeks truth through clarity of vision, an art that rejects comfort, ornament, luxury as unnecessary and probably dangerous distractions. Walter Benjamin writes:

> The talent of a good writer is to make use of his style to supply his thought with a spectacle of the kind provided by a well-trained body. He never says more than he has thought. Hence, his writing redounds not . . . to his own benefit, but solely to the benefit of what he wants to say.

To write only what you have thought is to bring a kind of materiality, or rather materialism (as in historical materialism), to your writing. The idealistic, the metaphysical, the fantastical, that which strives through leaps of faith and imagination for what is unknown—and perhaps unknowable, inarticulable—is forsaken. The work attains instead, as is indisputably the case in Kramer's plays, a powerful gravity, deeply rooted in the real.

It is through this materialism, which makes words "redound solely to the benefit" of a goal other than one's own aggrandizement, that *The Normal Heart* and *The Destiny of Me* escape self-hagiography, avoid all but the most generous, expansive narcissism. Kramer, like Shaw and Brecht, has forged a very public personality, a familiar voice and political stance through which his plays must be refracted by any reader or audience. The public Larry Kramer is virtually indistinguishable from the protagonist of his plays, Ned Weeks; even more than Shaw's Jack Tanner, Weeks is an author-surrogate, a Benjaminian "good writer" whose speech is almost entirely devoted to the cause he and his progenitor/creator hopes to advance. The language that, in these plays, creates the protagonist is a language ultimately dedicated to much more than any single self, and so the protagonist in question, Ned Weeks, is himself dedicated by the nature of the matter (language) of which he is composed, to the greater world, and the greater good. The title, *The Destiny of Me*, can, at first hearing, sound something like "Me! Me! Me!" The materiality of the language, however, as well as the dialectic that drives the play forward—the tensions between interior, intimate memory and exterior social transformation—turn the titular "Me" away from the self-regarding and solipsistic toward something huge and Whitmanesque—a democratic "Me" that is surrogate for "We," a paradoxically inclusive egoism, a self that is communal, shared.

The unornamented quality of the language, rooted in a desire for truth, in which desire is implicit a belief in the *existence* of truth, announces Kramer's Jewishness, notwithstanding his protestations in interviews that he is "a bad Jew" (in the sense of being nonbelieving). Although God and His promise of a better life hereafter may have been dismissed by Kramer as just another false comfort, the muscular directness of his writing, its spontaneous spoken-ness, its proud discomfort, its inelegant elegance, are Jewish tropes. Perhaps the rejection of the imagistic by certain Jewish writers originates in the Second Commandment's interdict against graven images, against representation. This is the voice of Torah, of Talmud, of the scrupulous, tireless parsing of Moral Law. Certainly Ned Weeks calls to mind, as has been often remarked about his author, of one of the prophets of the Holy Scriptures, an Amos, perhaps, torn equally between love and fury for his people, righteous indignation manifest as towering rage shot through with heartbreak, with unrequited but inextinguishable devotion.

Kramer's unadorned prose is evocative of the best Jewish-American writing: of Singer, Malamud, Bellow, Ozick, Roth, Kunitz, Paley. This is the speech of the newly arrived, the immigrant, the oppositionist, the pariah; it is underclass, or working class, or even middle-class. If it has any aristocratic bearing, this voice, this language belongs to an aristocracy of intellectual fearlessness, and never to one of social privilege. Insofar as this plain, tormented speech derives from an absolute, uncompromising fealty to the search for what is true, to the centrality of that search above all others, it is Jewish speech, deriving as well from the search's concomitant, the Jewish assumption that the truth is in fact graspable through an application of courage and will and intelligence. Larry Kramer's speech is Jewish in the devotion it displays to the messianic conviction that the truth liberates if its precepts are entirely engaged with, and lived.

This plainness of speech is not, it must be said, particularly gay. The quill wielded in the writing of these plays is neither cut from a feather nor dipped in an ink of any discernibly violet hue. Gay theater descends from the twin tributaries of Tennessee Williams on the "legitimate" side, and such artists as Jack Smith and Charles Ludlam on the demimondaine, distaff side. It cascades from the former in torrents of voluptuous, even delirious exclamation, and from the latter in an even more delirious reveling in the groves of inspired camp, dazzling with irony. Gay male literature descends from Oscar Wilde to Ronald Firbank to Edmund White to Dale Peck, gay male poetry from Whitman to Mark Doty, writers for whom long-breathed lines and intricately detailed surfaces are expressions of agency, are (for contemporary writers at least) a proud displaying and a public reclamation of identity, a rejection of shame, a manifestation of power. Larry Kramer's other major play, *Just Say No*, a wicked, giddy farce with a serious core, employs many of the exuberant gestures one associates with gay writing. If read in the context of the gay literature of its time, his superb novel *Faggots* only deviates from a comfortable, honorable niche in that genre when one understands the way in which its profoundly angry, moral core, whence, finally, something like prophecy begins to flow, seeks to cancel the book's generic membership—while at the same time its style and wit reaffirm its allegiances.

The Normal Heart or *The Destiny of Me* are unlike any gay drama that precedes them. For all that gay men are their principal, passionately addressed subject and object, at no point in either text does the playwright exploit the conventions of gay theater. The plays are never voluptuous, never ironic; every moment of tentative, awkward camp is batted away by pain, rage and sorrow as soon as it appears. Here are two of gay theater's most significant plays, but to find a voice to serve firmly as their antecedent, one must look outside the canon of gay literature and gay theater practice. One thinks of Eugene O'Neill, demanding that a theater believed capable merely of entertainment surrender its glamour and its magic spells and disfigure itself, if necessary, in a dive down to the bottom of the ocean, to find what exists there, to bring submerged reality up to light and air. O'Neill, and later Arthur Miller, are the forebears of a realist, anti-lyrical theater that bravely tosses aside the habiliments of conventional pleasure, seeking ever greater

depths. Under the pressures of the deep, language loses its melli-
fluence, its ease. Its compression bears witness to its strenuous, fearless diving. Near the conclusion of America's greatest play, *Long
Day's Journey into Night* (another play addressing, as Kramer's plays
do, life estranged, outside society and outside one's own family, and
also addressing the relationship of money to health care), Edmund
says: "Stammering is the native eloquence of us fog people." More
than classic, or Brechtian, or Jewish, the truest derivation of Larry
Kramer's diction in these plays can be traced back to the American
stage.

The plays of O'Neill have their political dimensions. Their
preoccupations with money, dislocation, vengeful memory, hollow
dreams are all American political themes. Still, it would be hard to
justify calling O'Neill a manifestly political writer, given his spiri-
tual obsessions, his theological questioning, his soul wrestling, the
specifically Christian agony that underlies most of his work.

Larry Kramer is a political writer. He has stated repeatedly
that formal aesthetic concerns are no great concern of his, that he
chooses different media (novel, screenplay, essay, play) depending
on which seems most useful at a given juncture to the accomplishment of an explicitly social goal. The break Kramer makes with gay
theater and the link he had forged with O'Neill and Miller in his
Weeks family plays are largely accidental, incidental to his purpose,
which is to effect social change.

The Normal Heart is profoundly political, a play in which a
momentous event in a man's life—falling in love for the first time,
harvesting on a personal level one of the sweetest fruits (so to speak)
of liberation, which is love—is overwhelmed by a historical event,
by the arrival of the plague, by the political crisis it engenders. The
insight, the political wisdom of the author of *The Normal Heart*, is
that he eschews the contemplative, speculative, idealist path to

wisdom and insight. In the face of a calamity, the play, appropriate
to its moment, is plunged by the playwright into action, into
political response. *The Normal Heart* is, in one sense, remarkably, a
play about fund-raising and organizing, and as such, in dramatic
literature, it is sui generis. Ned and Felix's love story contends for
center stage with and at many moments is crowded from the center by the onrush of the meta-personal, the external, by betrayal and
confusion and idiocy and cowardice and courage, by the shadow of
death on a holocaustal scale. In capturing the conflict occasioned
in an individual, and in all individuals, by political engagement on
the one hand and the private preserves of Eros on the other; the
conundrum posed by a clash between having social agency and a
social life; in depicting so savagely, accurately and honestly the
dilemma faced by people confronted by historical forces; by mas-
terfully and relentlessly colliding personal pathology against grand
historical misadventure, wisdom and insight are attained.

A blending of epic and lyric, epic and elegy, *The Normal Heart*
will endure long after the AIDS crisis has passed. It will survive
in the same way that *A Doll's House* has survived the world-altering
successes of the feminist revolution: the problematics of change,
human and historical change, have their constants, and Larry
Kramer's recognition and delineation of those constants will
endure.

The Normal Heart is transformed and deepened by being considered alongside *The Destiny of Me*, and vice versa. The first play ends
with a classical liberal utopian vision—again, note the earthbound
concreteness of this vision, its unembellished simplicity:

> Felix, when they invited me to Gay Week at Yale, they
> had a dance.... In my old college dining hall, just across cam-
> pus from that tiny freshman room where I wanted to kill myself

because I thought I was the only gay man in the world—they had a dance. Felix, there were six hundred young men and women there. Smart, exceptional young men and women . . .

The progress, real and anticipated, implicit in this passage has as its counterweight (or perhaps counterpunch would be more accurate) the bleak closing moments of *The Destiny of Me*, in which the past, in the form of a frightened, vulnerable child, asking his grizzled adult incarnation what his destiny is, is bequeathed a glimpse of a truly awful future:

> You're going to go to eleven shrinks. You won't fall in love for forty years. And when a nice man finally comes along and tries to teach you to love him and love yourself, he dies from a plague. Which is waiting to kill you, too.

This is cruel, and terrifying. A conditional survival, so morally ambiguous a goal, is the furthest look forward *Destiny* is willing to allow. The gratitude which is uttered like a prayer or a line from a love poem at the end of *Normal Heart* ("Thank you, Felix") has as its answer the deeply ambivalent declaration that closes *Destiny:* "I want to stay a little longer." Stay, but only a little longer.

The dialogue in *Destiny* between Ned and his younger incarnation, Alexander, suggests a porousness among present, future and past. The past looks to the present, as Walter Benjamin imagined, asking to be rescued, endowing the present with the power of rescue. If the enemy wins, if there is to be no victory, no triumph, everything is lost. "Not even the dead will be safe," Benjamin warns. *Destiny* stages what the living owe the dead, the past: rescue. The play also suggests, terrifyingly, that the rescue may not be forthcoming.

The two plays merge into a single work of literature. The invisible but electric presence of the offstage activists in *Destiny* offsets Weeks's despair, couched in his unresistant, beleaguered body, with their ongoing resistance and communally generated hope; and they are his "children." They are ACT UP, the glorious consequence of the brutal, costly battling witnessed in *Normal Heart*. The disappointments, misunderstandings, anathemas, backstabbings, all wretchedly inescapable in any organizing effort, have, by the time of *Destiny*, produced an army of warriors, "smart, exceptional young men and women." We are taught by this flowering of activism to doubt despair.

And we are also taught to anticipate despair, for the effort to remember has only, cruelly, resulted in the future managing to betray the past. The activists, Ned's children, cannot save him from the viral enemy inside; and Ned, ultimately, cannot offer Alexander the promise of a golden tomorrow. Transcending the personal miseries of the past may not result in future joy, and the fantastically successful effort to organize politically is routed by human foibles and worse, by science and the obstinacy of viral sublife.

Where else in dramatic literature is there such a treatment of the life-and-death cycle of people and political change? One needs to reach back to the chronicles of Shakespeare, back to the Greeks. Larry Kramer isn't Sophocles and he isn't Shakespeare; we don't have Sophocleses or Shakespeares, not these days, but we do have, on rare occasion, remarkable accomplishment, and Kramer's is remarkable, invaluable, and rare. How else to dramatize revolution accurately, truthfully, *politically*, than by showing it to be tragic as well as triumphant? And on the other hand, if the medical, biological, political, and familial failures of *Destiny* produce, by the play's end, despair again; if we are plunged back into night, it cannot be different from the night with which *Normal Heart* began, rife with despair and terror, and pregnant with an offstage potential for transformation, for hope.

Failure awaits any political movement, even a spectacularly successful movement such as the one Larry Kramer helped to spark and organize. Political movements, liberation movements, revolutions, are as subject to time, decline, mortality, tragedy as any human enterprise, or any human being. Death waits for every living thing, no matter how vital or brilliant its accomplishment; death waits for people and for their best and worst efforts as well. Politics is a living thing, and living things die. The mistake is to imagine otherwise, to believe that progress doesn't generate as many new problems as it generates blessings, to imagine, foolishly, that the struggle can be won decisively, finally, definitively. No matter what any struggle accomplishes, time, life, death bring in their changes, and new oppressions are always forming from the ashes of the old. The fight for justice, for a better world, for civil rights or access to medicine, is a never-ending fight, at least as far as we have sight to see. The full-blooded description of this truth, the recognition and dramatization of a political cycle of birth, death, rebirth, defeat, renewal—this is true tragedy, in which absolute loss and devastation, *Nothing,* is arrived at, and from this Nothing, something new is born. This tragic vision is perhaps the true, unique genius of these plays.

2.

The Destiny of Me rounds out and completes *The Normal Heart* with redemptive moments of an understanding that brings forgiveness—forgiveness, not release, not freedom from pain. Nothing in the plays is more moving or more compelling than Kramer's unflinching portrait of his two impossible parents, so unforgivable, so inexcusable, so much the victims and the victimizers, all at once. When Ned expresses too much sympathy for his abusive father, his younger self reprimands him, and the audience: "Don't you dare feel sorry for him!" And don't you dare not to. The author of *The Normal Heart* and *The Destiny of Me* was badly abused by psychoanalysts and has many unkind things to say about psychoanalysis, but he is clearly its creature as well as one of its many critics. His search for the truth is that of the talented analysand's. The poet H.D., in her *Tribute to Freud*, wrote about her psychoanalysis as a matter of life-and-death striving toward transformation:

> . . . I have the feeling of holding my breath under water. As if I were searching under water for some priceless treasure, and if I bobbed up to the surface the clue of its whereabouts would be lost forever. So I, though seated upright, am in a sense diving, head-down, underwater—in another element, and as I seem now so near to getting the answer or finding the treasure, I feel that my whole life, my whole being, will be blighted forever if I miss this chance. I must not lose my grip, I must not lose the end of the picture and so miss the meaning of the whole, so far painfully perceived. I must hold on here or the picture will blur over and the sequence will be lost. In a sense, it seems that I am drowning; already half-drowned to the ordinary dimensions of space and time, I know that I must drown, as it were, completely in order to come out on the other side of things (like Alice with her looking-glass or Perseus with his mirror). I must drown and come out on the other side, or rise to the surface after the third time down, not dead to this life but with a new set of values, my treasure dredged from the depth. I must be born again or break utterly.

The protean Alexander/Ned, name and identity tossed about by all manner of tempests, nearly breaks, and both is and is not born again; or rather, is born again, but born again surrounded by ghosts, born again into a horrible dying. In their ardent pursuit of memory and understanding, in their simultaneous optimism and pessimism, the Weeks-family plays are genuinely Freudian tragedy. One drowns to come out on the other side. Annihilation brings new life.

I remember, when I saw *Destiny* at the Lucille Lortel Theater in the winter of 1992, one moment I found jaw-dropping: when Ned, observer/participant in his bygone family drama, admonishes his mother, the great and terrible Rena, parading in a slip and bra:

NED: Ma, why don't you put on a dress?
RENA: If you're going to become a writer, you must learn to be
    more precise with words.
NED: Do not sit half-naked with your adolescent son. Is that
    precise enough?

It's a brilliant, complicated moment, funny and very sad. It occurs just when this fierce, unhappy woman is talking about "how impossible it is for a woman to be independent." She is reaching for nascent consciousness, toward her own liberation. In the context of the political drama, her frustration and sense of injustice feed her young son, his surprising, even happy self-assurance in the present and the fighter he will become. The character of Ned-as-a-boy, Alexander, is his mother's champion. But in the context of the family drama, her battle for liberation is threatening, disruptive, it's one more aspect of a personality too large for the role she's been forced into, a woman who can't accept boundaries. Her energy, her anger, her lack of boundaries—including perhaps sexual and familial ones—

will coruscate those she loves. The man her son will become, aware after the fact of the damage she's doing even while bestowing the gift of agency, undercuts her, pathologizes her—not necessarily without cause or merit, but all the same she is undercut.

There are ambiguities, fallacies, in Rena's externalized sense of her oppression—this is, after all, *after* World War II, it isn't the nineteenth century, she isn't Nora, and she's sort of crazy. So too are there ambiguities and injustice in Ned's chastisement. Is she being politically sabotaged to secure the family? *Is* she behaving inappropriately? I don't know how to answer that, but the moment is a good one because it makes me squirm. My jaw dropped at the chutzpah of the lines, the sudden intimacy. The character/playwright is betraying his mother, not only her ambitions but her privacy, his family's secrets. He is even, in a sense, transgressing against his larger family, the gay community, implying, or at the very least risking the misreading, that in Ned's complaint is the etiology of his sexual orientation, a very risky implication these days, but again, not without at least enough conditional, circumspective plausibility to merit its staging, if one has the courage, the nerve to do so.

(And no, I do *not* believe that seductive mommies make gay sons; but I do believe that the family romance has some part in shaping sexual desire, gay, straight or otherwise. And any allusion to this truth, in the Age of the Genome, makes me happy.)

Rena is saying what is very hard to say politically, and more than she intends personally; Ned is saying what is hard to say personally, and more than he intends politically; and it would be nice if what we need would always coincide with what was good for us, or with what was generous or just, but there are always these discrepancies. The playwright leaves the engine running, resolving nothing, not forcing resolution on what cannot be resolved, on what is tragic, allowing the tragic to generate new syntheses. Time brings on its changes. Liberation, personal or political, even attained, is not an end, a point of arrival, but a point of departure, a step toward something new.

3.

Time works its changes, and at any given point in his life, Larry Kramer is being abused as a left-wing hysteric or deplored as a right-wing antisex scold. He is impressively unconcerned, at least publicly, with the constant stream of opprobrium sent in his direction, and in fact rather (in)famously invites it; he is one of the few remaining public intellectuals who is willing and eager to brawl. He has paid a high personal price for the brawling. It has cost him much time, and probably great sorrow and fear. The sacrifice of time and emotional life for the sake of inflaming and expanding public debate is a rare thing in a writer in this day and age, a sacrifice too seldom recognized and honored, too often shrugged off as a well-deserved comeuppance.

What seems to matter most to Larry Kramer is the incessant disruption of business as usual, the refusal to be silent or polite. This refusal is praiseworthy. It is only to be expected that any person so completely engaged, so entirely committed to action (and discourse as he discourses is a potent form of action) will make mistakes, will enrage and appall. Given the sheer amount of engagement, of public declaration, it is astounding how often history and reality have affirmed what Kramer has proposed.

His campaign against the oversexualization of gay male life, against indiscriminate, profligate fucking, in favor of long-term commitment (the antimonogamist riposte to which preference, by the way, is given a fair amount of eloquent stage time in *Normal Heart*) has caused a good deal of unhappiness in our community, as one learns simply by reading the plays. This campaign of Kramer's is, in my opinion, a brave opening gambit in the pursuit of what must surely be the next step after sexual revolution and liberation, namely the articulation of a new ethics of sexuality. The revolution isn't over and liberation has not yet arrived, but looking ahead to the next step after the triumph of our efforts cannot be considered premature. It is, rather, essential—for without a forward vision, how are we to progress? The monogamy-versus-promiscuity model is clearly inadequate to our purposes, and if Kramer relies too heavily on such a model, then criticism is appropriate, but not a rejection of his anguished call for personal responsibility.

The homosexual right, pretending that the homosexual revolution has not been a *sexual* revolution, uses "personal responsibility," or rather an imaginary lack thereof, as a canard with which to discredit the homosexual left. Dividing the community into the "personally responsible" and the "sexually misbehaving," gay and lesbian conservatives seek to desexualize sexual orientation, to locate the cause of our general disenfranchisement in what they bemoan as the lack of propriety, decency, maturity, sobriety, "family values" manifest in some undesirable percentage of our population—a percentage that happens to coincide, in the writings of the right, precisely with the percentage of our community that is activist and left. These revisionists want to rewrite our liberation as a begging for, and *perhaps* a slow granting of, a place at the table of power. They want to demote our history of effective, collective, militant action to the status of sideshow, a distraction from the real work conducted in private meetings by well-heeled, well-placed conservative individuals—hoping thereby to earn shiny credentials to flash at Republican conventions and other assemblages of virulent homophobes. With "personal responsibility" as their battle cry, the gay and lesbian right seeks to remove homosexual enfranchisement from its place as a chapter in the book of liberation and paste it squarely in the book of the irresistible rise of entrepreneurial individualism.

But Larry Kramer's invocation of personal responsibility is not consonant with theirs. Kramer's demand that we save ourselves, that we take responsibility for ourselves, is historically, communally based. His is a demand always accompanied by a powerful depiction of its context—historical, and ongoing, homophobia, life-threatening oppression, which he has time and again (and in both of these plays) likened to the holocaust. Kramer has declared the homophobia behind the wide world's response to the AIDS epidemic a great crime against humanity, and in doing so he has renamed the ostensibly biological as actually political. This act of renaming, this exposing of ideology, is antithetical to the practices and program of the political right.

Kramer is telling us *we must save ourselves*. He is forcefully reminding us that being the object of hatred for millennia will make any subject hate her- or himself. He is demanding that, as we liberate ourselves, we also tranform what we are liberating, that we rid ourselves of self-hatred and begin the riddance by naming it. But he has never through all this hectoring lost sight of the fact that we are more hated than self-hating, that we are in a fight with an enemy whose implacable detestation of us is the true nemesis against which our battles are waged. The two plays collected here are magnificent examples of this understanding, which by virtue of its historicity, its complexity, its realism, is unmistakably progressive.

We'll go down if we don't stand up for ourselves.

Surely you see that.

If Larry Kramer makes you angry, he also has a rich claim on your forgiveness. Read these plays.

4.

The Washington Weekses, like the New England Tyrones, and their nearly coeval Brooklyn equivalents the Lomans, are "fog people"; you can tell by the way they talk. Their eloquence is all in the hesitations, in the tumult. They are most patently American in this, that they betray in every word and gesture how densely the fog surrounds them, how nearly impossible it is to move forward. Doubts, confusions, night sweats, real darkness: a fog has hovered about and haunted every moment of American history, potential doom obscuring potential illumination. The fog pours in to engulf any great work, any new beginning, any attempt to overturn and start anew, any voyage past what is known. Progress is unimaginably difficult, dangerous, always at risk, always made by people with only partial vision. American actors, historical, familial, political, theatrical, move blindly ahead toward a future that never is, and never can be, clear. The great error has been to mistake the darkness for damnation, to surrender to immobility or worse, to try to retrace our steps backward to a safety that has ceased to exist or never existed. It is nearly impossible to move forward. And yet move forward is precisely what the courageous among the fog people do.

Here is an American epic, a wandering without a homecoming. We haven't aged sufficiently as a community, or as a nation, even to imagine what the homecoming will be like. The doom that haunts every American epic is here made manifest in a plague, which has now grown to globally holocaustal dimensions: fifty million infected, sixteen million dead, ten percent increases in new infections every year. And still there is no cure, still there is mendacity and calumny and malign neglect and hatred for the Other— gay, female, black, brown, yellow, non-American, poor. And still there are the epic virtues, still there is astonishing courage, generosity, nobility and heroism, still the grand battles to change the world and the order of things, still the refusal to accept inujustice, blind destiny, even fate. This doom and these virtues are given full-blooded stage life in *The Normal Heart* and *The Destiny of Me*. Together the plays constitute an American epic, improbably and perhaps accidentally of the theater. Their vision is individual and deeply communal. It is tragic and unceasingly generative. Its characters are possessed of a stammering eloquence, and what they speak is uncomfortable, outrageous, abrasive, brave: the truth. These plays give the lie to a theater of diminished expectations and humbled ambitions. Here is theater that has managed to matter, the work of a deep-diving heart as hot as the sun.

—Tony Kushner
New York City
June 2000

The Normal Heart

For Norman J. Levy,
who succeeded where all others failed.

The windiest militant trash
Important Persons shout
Is not so crude as our wish:
What mad Nijinsky wrote
About Diaghilev
Is true of the normal heart;
For the error bred in the bone
Of each woman and each man
Craves what it cannot have,
Not universal love
But to be loved alone.

All I have is a voice
To undo the folded lie,
The romantic lie in the brain
Of the sensual man-in-the-street
And the lie of Authority
Whose buildings grope the sky:
There is no such thing as the State
And no one exists alone;
Hunger allows no choice
To the citizen or the police;
We must love one another or die.

From "September 1, 1939"
W. H. Auden

Acknowledgments

Theater is an especially collaborative endeavor. Many people help to make a play.

I would like to thank: Arthur Kramer (as always), A. J. Antoon, Ann and Don Brown, Michael Callen, Michael Carlisle, Joseph Chaikin, Kate Costello, Dr. James D'Eramo, Helen Eisenbach, Dr. Roger Enlow, Tom Erhardt, Robert Ferro, Emmett Foster, Jim Fouratt, Sanford Friedman, Dr. Alvin Friedman-Kien, Dr. Patrick Hennessey, Richard Howard, Jane Isay, Dr. Richard Isay, Chuck Jones, Owen Laster, Dr. Frank Lilly, Joan and David Maxwell, Rodger McFarlane, Patrick Merla, Hermine and Maurice Nessen, Mike Nichols, Nick Olcott, Charles Ortleb, Johnnie Planco, Judy Prince, Margaret Ramsay, Mary Anne and Douglas Schwalbe, Will Schwalbe, Dr. Joseph Sonnabend, and Tim Westmoreland.

I particularly thank my intelligent cast, and our director, Michael Lindsay-Hogg, a humble, gentle man of great patience and courage.

I give special thanks and tribute to Dr. Linda J. Laubenstein.

I am grateful to the following works of scholarship: "American Jewry During the Holocaust," a report edited by Seymour Maxwell Finger for the American Jewish Commission on the Holocaust, Hon. Arthur J. Goldberg, Chairman, March 1984 (the excerpt quoted herein is used by permission); *Israel in the Mind of America* by Peter Grose, Alfred A. Knopf, 1983; *American Jewry's Public Re-*

sponse to the Holocaust, 1938–44: An Examination Based upon Accounts in the Jewish Press and Periodical Literature, A Doctoral Dissertation by Haskel Lookstein, Yeshiva University, January 1979, University Microfilms, Ann Arbor, Michigan; *While Six Million Died: A Chronicle of American Apathy,* by Arthur D. Morse, copyright © 1967, The Overlook Press, Woodstock, New York, 1983; *The Abandonment of the Jews: America and the Holocaust, 1941–1945,* by David S. Wyman, Pantheon Books, 1984.

For encouraging, challenging, inspiring, and teaching me—for caring—I am exceptionally indebted to Gail Merrifield, the Director of Plays at the New York Shakespeare Festival, as I am to this remarkable organization's Literary Manager, Bill Hart.

Indeed, there is not a person at the New York Shakespeare Festival to whom I cannot say, Thank you.

There are no words splendid enough to contain and convey what Joseph Papp has meant to me, and to this play.

There are many people who lived this play, who lived these years, and who live no more. I miss them.

—*Larry Kramer*

The original New York production of *The Normal Heart* opened on April 21, 1985 at the Public Theater in New York City, New York; a New York Shakespeare Festival Production, it was produced by Joseph Papp. It had the following cast:

Cast of Characters

(in order of appearance)

Craig Donner Michael Santoro
Mickey Marcus Robert Dorfman
Ned Weeks Brad Davis
David Lawrence Lott
Dr. Emma Brookner Concetta Tomei
Bruce Niles David Allen Brooks
Felix Turner D. W. Moffett
Ben Weeks Phillip Richard Allen
Tommy Boatwright William DeAcutis
Hiram Keebler Lawrence Lott
Grady Micbael Santoro
Examining Doctor Lawrence Lott
Orderly Lawrence Lott
Orderly Michael Santoro

Director Michael Lindsay-Hogg
Scenery Eugene Lee and Keith Raywood
Lighting Natasha Katz
Costumes Bill Walker
Associate Producer Jason Steven Cohen

The action of this play takes place between July 1981 and May 1984 in New York City.

Scenes and Approximate Dates

Act One

Act Two

About the Production

The New York Shakespeare Festival production at the Public Theater was conceived as exceptionally simple. Little furniture was used: a few wooden office chairs, a desk, a table, a sofa, and an old battered hospital gurney that found service as an examining table, a bench in City Hall, and a place for coats in the organization's old office. As the furniture found itself doing double-duty in different scenes, so did the doorways built into the set's back wall. In many instances, the actors used the theater itself for entrances and exits.

The walls of the set, made of construction-site plywood, were whitewashed. Everywhere possible, on this set and upon the theater walls too, facts and figures and names were painted, in black, simple lettering.

Here are some of the things we painted on our walls:

1. Principal place was given to the latest total number of AIDS cases nationally: _____ AND COUNTING. (For example, on August 1, 1985, the figure read 12,062.)

    As the Centers for Disease Control revise all figures regularly, so did we, crossing out old numbers and placing the new figure just beneath it.

2. This was also done for states and major cities.

3. EPIDEMIC OFFICIALLY DECLARED JUNE 5, 1981.
4. MAYOR KOCH: $75,000—MAYOR FEINSTEIN: $16,000,000. (For public education and community services.)
5. "TWO MILLION AMERICANS ARE INFECTED— ALMOST 10 TIMES THE OFFICIAL ESTIMATES"— Dr. Robert Gallo, London *Observer*, April 7, 1985.
6. The number of cases in children.
7. The number of cases in gays and the number of cases in straights, calculated by subtracting the gay and bisexual number from the total CDC figure.
8. The total number of articles on the epidemic written by the following newspapers during the first ten months of 1984:

    The *San Francisco Chronicle* 163
    The *New York Times* 41
    The *Los Angeles Times* 37
    The *Washington Post* 24

9. During the first nineteen months of the epidemic, the *New York Times* wrote about it a total of seven times:

    1. July 3, 1981, page 20 (41 cases reported by CDC)
    2. August 29, 1981, page 9 (107 cases)
    3. May 11, 1982, Section III, page 1 (335 cases)
    4. June 18, 1982, Section II, page 8 (approximately 430 cases)
    5. August 8, 1982, page 31 (505 cases)
    6. January 6, 1983, Section II, page 17 (approximately 891 cases)
    7. February 6, 1983, Magazine (the "Craig Claiborne" article) (958 cases)

10. During the three months of the Tylenol scare in 1982, the
    New York Times wrote about it a total of 54 times:

    October 1, 2, 3, 4, 5, 6, 7, 8, 9, 10, 11, 12, 13, 14, 15, 16, 17,
    18, 19, 20, 21, 22, 23, 24, 25, 26, 27, 28, 29, 30, 31

    November 2, 5, 6, 9, 12, 17, 21, 22, 25

    December 1, 2, 3, 4, 8, 10, 14, 15, 19, 25, 27, 28, 29, 30

    Four of these articles appeared on the front page.

    Total number of cases: 7.

11. Government research at the National Institutes of Health
    did not commence in reality until January 1983, eighteen
    months after the same government had declared the
    epidemic.

12. One entire wall contained this passage:

    "There were two alternative strategies a Jewish orga-
    nization could adopt to get the American government to
    initiate action on behalf of the imperiled Jews of Europe.
    It could cooperate with the government officials, quietly
    trying to convince them that rescue of Jews should be one
    of the objectives of the war, or it could try to pressure the
    government into initiating rescue by using embarrassing
    public attention and rallying public opinion to that end.

    The American Jewish Committee chose the former
    strategy and clung to it tenaciously.

    From the very onset of Jewish crises, the Committee
    responded to each new Nazi outrage by practicing their
    traditional style of discreet 'backstairs' diplomacy.

    With each worsening event, the Committee reacted by
    contacting yet another official or re-visiting the same ones
    to call their attention to the new situation.

The Jewish delegates were usually politely informed that the matter was being given the 'most earnest attention.'

They were still trying to persuade the same officials when the war ended."

From "American Jewry During the Holocaust," Prepared for the American Jewish Commission on the Holocaust, 1984, Edited by Seymour Maxwell Finger

13. Announcement of the discovery of "the virus" in France: January 1983.

   Announcement of the "discovery" of "the virus" in Washington: April 1984.

14. The public education budget for 1985 at the U.S. Department of Health and Human Services: $120,000.

15. Vast expanses of wall were covered with lists of names, much like the names one might find on a war memorial, such as the Vietnam Memorial in Washington.

Foreword

Larry Kramer's *The Normal Heart* is a play in the great tradition of Western drama. In taking a burning social issue and holding it up to public and private scrutiny so that it reverberates with the social and personal implications of that issue, *The Normal Heart* reveals its origins in the theater of Sophocles, Euripides, and Shakespeare. In his moralistic fervor, Larry Kramer is a first cousin to nineteenth-century Ibsen and twentieth-century Odets and other radical writers of the 1930s. Yet, at the heart of *The Normal Heart*, the element that gives this powerful political play its essence, is love—love holding firm under fire, put to the ultimate test, facing and overcoming our greatest fear: death.

I love the ardor of this play, its howling, its terror and its kindness. It makes me very proud to be its producer and caretaker.

—Joseph Papp

Act One

Scene 1

The office of DR. EMMA BROOKNER. *Three men are in the waiting area:* CRAIG DONNER, MICKEY MARCUS, *and* NED WEEKS.

CRAIG: (*After a long moment of silence.*) I know something's wrong.

MICKEY: There's nothing wrong. When you're finished we'll go buy you something nice. What would you like?

CRAIG: We'll go somewhere nice to eat, okay? Did you see that guy in there's spots?

MICKEY: You don't have those. Do you?

CRAIG: No.

MICKEY: Then you don't have anything to worry about.

CRAIG: She said they can be inside you, too.

MICKEY: They're not inside you.

CRAIG: They're inside me.

MICKEY: Will you stop! Why are you convinced you're sick?

CRAIG: Where's Bruce? He's supposed to be here. I'm so lucky to have such a wonderful lover. I love Bruce so much, Mickey. I know something's wrong.

19

MICKEY: Craig, all you've come for is some test results. Now stop being such a hypochondriac.

CRAIG: I'm tired all the time. I wake up in swimming pools of sweat. Last time she felt me and said I was swollen. I'm all swollen, like something ready to explode. Thank you for coming with me, you're a good friend. Excuse me for being such a mess, Ned. I get freaked out when I don't feel well.

MICKEY: Everybody does.

(DAVID *comes out of* EMMA's *office. There are highly visible purple lesions on his face. He wears a long-sleeved shirt. He goes to get his jacket, which he's left on one of the chairs.*)

DAVID: Whoever's next can go in.

CRAIG: Wish me luck.

MICKEY: (*Hugging* CRAIG.) Good luck.

(CRAIG *hugs him, then* NED, *and goes into* EMMA's *office.*)

DAVID: They keep getting bigger and bigger and they don't go away. (*To* NED.) I sold you a ceramic pig once at Maison France on Bleecker Street. My name is David.

NED: Yes, I remember. Somebody I was friends with then collects pigs and you had the biggest pig I'd ever seen outside of a real pig.

DAVID: I'm her twenty-eighth case and sixteen of them are dead. (*He leaves.*)

NED: Mickey, what the fuck is going on?

MICKEY: I don't know. Are you here to write about this?

NED: I don't know. What's wrong with that?

MICKEY: Nothing, I guess.

NED: What about you? What are you going to say? You're the one with the health column.

MICKEY: Well, I'll certainly write about it in the *Native,* but I'm afraid to put it in the stuff I write at work.

NED: What are you afraid of?

MICKEY: The city doesn't exactly show a burning interest in gay health. But at least I've still got my job: the Health Department has had a lot of cutbacks.

NED: How's John?

MICKEY: John? John who?

NED: You've had so many I never remember their last names.

MICKEY: Oh, you mean John. I'm with Gregory now. Gregory O'Connor.

NED: The old gay activist?

MICKEY: Old? He's younger than you are. I've been with Gregory for ten months now.

NED: Mickey, that's very nice.

MICKEY: He's not even Jewish. But don't tell my rabbi.

CRAIG: (*Coming out of* EMMA'*s office.*) I'm going to die. That's the bottom line of what she's telling me. I'm so scared. I have to go home and get my things and come right back and check in. Mickey, please come with me. I hate hospitals. I'm going to die. Where's Bruce? I want Bruce.

(MICKEY *and* CRAIG *leave.* DR. EMMA BROOKNER *comes in from her office. She is in a motorized wheelchair. She is in her mid-to-late thirties.*)

EMMA: Who are you?

NED: I'm Ned Weeks. I spoke with you on the phone after the *Times* article.

EMMA: You're the writer fellow who's scared. I'm scared, too. I hear you've got a big mouth.

NED: Is big mouth a symptom?

EMMA: No, a cure. Come on in and take your clothes off.

(*Lights up on an examining table, center stage.* NED *starts to undress.*)

NED: Dr. Brookner, what's happening?

EMMA: I don't know.

NED: In just a couple of minutes you told two people I know something. The article said there isn't any cure.

EMMA: Not even any good clues yet. And even if they found out tomorrow what's happening, it takes years to find out how to cure and prevent anything. All I know is this disease is the most insidious killer I've ever seen or studied or heard about. And I think we're seeing only the tip of the iceberg. And I'm afraid it's on the rampage. I'm frightened nobody important is going to give a damn because it seems to be happening mostly to gay men. Who cares if a faggot dies? Does it occur to you to do anything about it. Personally?

NED: Me?

EMMA: Somebody's got to do something.

NED: Wouldn't it be better coming from you?

EMMA: Doctors are extremely conservative; they try to stay out of anything that smells political, and this smells. Bad. As soon as you start screaming you get treated like a nut case. Maybe you know that. And then you're ostracized and rendered worthless, just when you need cooperation most. Take off your socks.

(NED, *in his undershorts, is now sitting on the examining table.* EMMA *will now examine him, his skin particularly, starting with the bottom of his feet, feeling his lymph glands, looking at his scalp, into his mouth . . .*)

NED: Nobody listens for very long anyway. There's a new disease of the month every day.

EMMA: This hospital sent its report of our first cases to the medical journals over a year ago. *The New England Journal of Medicine* has finally published it, and last week, which brought you running, the *Times* ran something on some inside page. Very inside: page twenty. If you remember, Legionnaires' Disease, toxic-shock, they both hit the front page of the *Times* the minute they happened. And stayed there until somebody did something. The front page of the *Times* has a way of inspiring action. Lie down.

NED: They won't even use the word "gay" unless it's in a direct quote. To them we're still homosexuals. That's like still calling blacks Negroes. The *Times* has always had trouble writing about anything gay.

EMMA: Then how is anyone going to know what's happening? And what precautions to take? Someone's going to have to tell the gay population fast.

NED: You've been living with this for over a year? Where's the mayor? Where's the Health Department?

EMMA: They know about it. You have a Commissioner of Health who got burned with the Swine Flu epidemic, declaring an emergency when there wasn't one. The government appropriated $150 million for that mistake. You have a mayor who's a bachelor and I assume afraid of being perceived as too friendly to anyone gay. And who is also out to protect a billion-dollar-a-year tourist industry. He's not about to tell the world there's an epidemic menacing his city. And don't ask me about the President. Is the mayor gay?

NED: If he is, like J. Edgar Hoover, who would want him?

EMMA: Have you had any of the symptoms?

NED: I've had most of the sexually transmitted diseases the article said come first. A lot of us have. You don't know what it's been like since the sexual revolution hit this country. It's been crazy, gay or straight.

EMMA: What makes you think I don't know? Any fever, weight loss, night sweats, diarrhea, swollen glands, white patches in your mouth, loss of energy, shortness of breath, chronic cough?

NED: No. But those could happen with a lot of things, couldn't they?

EMMA: And purple lesions. Sometimes. Which is what I'm looking for. It's a cancer. There seems to be a strange reaction in the immune system. It's collapsed. Won't work. Won't fight. Which is what it's supposed to do. So most of the diseases my guys are coming down with—and there are some very strange ones—are caused by germs that wouldn't hurt a baby, not a baby in New York City anyway. Unfortunately, the immune system is the system we know least about. So where is this big mouth I hear you've got?

NED: I have more of a bad temper than a big mouth.

EMMA: Nothing wrong with that. Plenty to get angry about. Health is a political issue. Everyone's entitled to good medical care. If you're not getting it, you've got to fight for it. Do you know this is the only country in the industrialized world besides South Africa that doesn't guarantee health care for everyone? Open your mouth. Turn over. One of my staff told me you were well-known in the gay world and not afraid to say what you think. Is that true? I can't find any gay leaders. I tried calling several gay organizations. No one ever calls me back. Is anyone out there?

NED: There aren't any organizations strong enough to be useful, no. Dr. Brookner, nobody with a brain gets involved in gay politics. It's filled with the great unwashed radicals of any counterculture. That's why there aren't any leaders the majority will follow. Anyway, you're talking to the wrong person. What I think is politically incorrect.

EMMA: Why?

NED: Gay is good to that crowd, no matter what. There's no room for criticism, looking at ourselves critically.

EMMA: What's your main criticism?

NED: I hate how we play victim, when many of us, most of us, don't have to.

EMMA: Then you're exactly what's needed now.

NED: Nobody ever listens. We're not exactly a bunch that knows how to play follow the leader.

EMMA: Maybe they're just waiting for somebody to lead them.

NED: We are. What group isn't?

EMMA: You can get dressed. I can't find what I'm looking for.

NED: (*Jumping down and starting to dress.*) Needed? Needed for what? What is it exactly you're trying to get me to do?

EMMA: Tell gay men to stop having sex.

NED: What?

EMMA: Someone has to. Why not you?

NED: It is a preposterous request.

EMMA: It only sounds harsh. Wait a few more years, it won't sound so harsh.

NED: Do you realize that you are talking about millions of men who have singled out promiscuity to be their principal political agenda, the one they'd die before abandoning. How do you deal with that?

EMMA: Tell them they may die.

NED: You tell them!

EMMA: Are you saying you guys can't relate to each other in a non-sexual way?

NED: It's more complicated than that. For a lot of guys it's not easy to meet each other in any other way. It's a way of connecting—which becomes an addiction. And then they're caught in the web of peer pressure to perform and perform. Are you sure this is spread by having sex?

EMMA: Long before we isolated the hepatitis viruses we knew about the diseases they caused and had a good idea of how they got around. I think I'm right about this. I am seeing more cases each week than the week before. I figure that by the end of the year the number will be doubling every six months. That's something over a thousand cases by next June. Half of them will be dead. Your two friends I've just diagnosed? One of them will be dead. Maybe both of them.

NED: And you want me to tell every gay man in New York to stop having sex?

EMMA: Who said anything about just New York?

NED: You want me to tell every gay man across the country—

EMMA: Across the world! That's the only way this disease will stop spreading.

NED: Dr. Brookner, isn't that just a tiny bit unrealistic?

EMMA: Mr. Weeks, if having sex can kill you, doesn't anybody with half a brain stop fucking? But perhaps you've never lost anything. Good-bye.

BRUCE: (*Calling from off.*) Where do I go? Where do I go?

(BRUCE NILES, *an exceptionally handsome man in his late thirties, rushes in carrying* CRAIG, *helped by* MICKEY.)

EMMA: Quickly—put him on the table. What happened?

BRUCE: He was coming out of the building and he started running to me and then he . . . then he collapsed to the ground.

EMMA: What is going on inside your bodies!

(CRAIG *starts to convulse.* BRUCE, MICKEY, *and* NED *restrain him.*)

EMMA: Gently. Hold on to his chin.

(*She takes a tongue depressor and holds* CRAIG'*s tongue flat; she checks the pulse in his neck; she looks into his eyes for vital signs that he is coming around;* CRAIG'*s convulsions stop.*)

You the lover?

BRUCE: Yes.

EMMA: What's your name?

BRUCE: Bruce Niles, ma'am.

EMMA: How's your health?

BRUCE: Fine. Why—is it contagious?

EMMA: I think so.

MICKEY: Then why haven't you come down with it?

EMMA: (*Moving toward a telephone.*) Because it seems to have a very long incubation period and require close intimacy. Niles? You were Reinhard Holz's lover?

BRUCE: How did you know that? I haven't seen him in a couple of years.

EMMA: (*Dialing the hospital emergency number.*) He died three weeks ago. Brookner. Emergency. Set up a room immediately.

(*Hangs up.*)

BRUCE: We were only boyfriends for a couple months.

MICKEY: It's like some sort of plague.

EMMA: There's always a plague. Of one kind or another. I've had it since I was a kid. Mr. Weeks, I don't think your friend is going to live for very long.

Scene 2

FELIX TURNER'S *desk at the* New York Times. FELIX *is always conservatively dressed, and is outgoing and completely masculine.*

NED: (*Entering, a bit uncomfortable and nervous.*) Mr. Turner?

FELIX: Bad timing. (*Looking up.*) "Mister"?

NED: My name is Ned Weeks.

FELIX: You caught me at a rough moment. I have a deadline.

NED: I've been told you're gay and might be able to help get vital information in the *Times* about—

FELIX: You've been told? Who told you?

NED: The grapevine.

FELIX: Here I thought everyone saw me as the Burt Reynolds of West Forty-third Street. Please don't stop by and say hello to Mr. Sulzberger or Abe Rosenthal. What kind of vital information?

NED: You read the article about this new disease?

FELIX: Yes, I read it. I wondered how long before I'd hear from somebody. Why does everyone gay always think I run the *New York Times*? I can't help you . . . with this.

NED: I'm sorry to hear that. What would you suggest I do?

FELIX: Take your pick. I've got twenty-three parties, fourteen gallery openings, thirty-seven new restaurants, twelve new discos, one hundred and five spring collections ... Anything sound interesting?

NED: No one here wants to write another article. I've talked to half a dozen reporters and editors and the guy who wrote the first piece.

FELIX: That's true. They won't want to write about it. And I can't. We're very departmentalized. You wouldn't want science to write about sweaters, would you?

NED: It is a very peculiar feeling having to go out and seek support from the straight world for something gay.

FELIX: I wouldn't know about that. I just write about gay designers and gay discos and gay chefs and gay rock stars and gay photographers and gay models and gay celebrities and gay everything. I just don't call them gay. Isn't that enough for doing my bit?

NED: No—I don't think it's going to be.

FELIX: I really do have a deadline and you wouldn't like me to get fired; who would write about us at all?

NED: Guys like you give me a pain in the ass. (*He starts out.*)

FELIX: Are you in the book?

NED: Yes.

Scene 3

The law office of BEN WEEKS, NED's *older brother.* BEN *always dresses in a suit and tie, which* NED *never does. The brothers love each other a great deal;* BEN's *approval is essential to* NED. BEN *is busy with some papers as* NED, *sitting on the opposite side of the desk, waits for him.*

BEN: Isn't it a bit early to get so worked up?

NED: Don't you be like that, too?

BEN: What have I done now?

NED: My friend Bruce and I went out to Fire Island and over the whole Labor Day weekend we collected the grand sum of $124.

BEN: You can read that as either an indication that it's a beginning and will improve, or as a portent that heads will stay in the sand. My advice is heads are going to stay in the sand.

NED: Because so many gay people are still in the closet?

BEN: Because people don't like to be frightened. When they get scared they don't behave well. It's called denial. (*Giving* NED *some papers to sign.*)

NED: (*Signs them automatically.*) What are these for?

BEN: Your account needs some more money. You never seem to do anything twice. One movie, one novel, one play . . . You know you are now living on your capital. I miss your being in the movie business. I like movies. (*Unrolls some blueprints.*)

NED: What are those?

BEN: I've decided to build a house.

NED: But the one you're in is terrific.

BEN: I just want to build me a dream house, so now I'm going to.

NED: It looks like a fortress. Does it have a moat? How much is it going to cost?

BEN: I suspect it'll wind up over a million bucks. But you're not to tell that to anyone. Not even Sara. I've found some land in Greenwich, by a little river, completely protected by trees. Ned, it's going to be beautiful.

NED: Doesn't spending a million dollars on a house frighten you? It would scare the shit out of me. Even if I had it.

BEN: You can have a house anytime you want one. You haven't done badly.

NED: Do I detect a tinge of approval—from the big brother who always called me lemon?

BEN: Well, you were a lemon.

NED: I don't want a house.

BEN: Then why have you been searching for one in the country for so many years?

NED: It's no fun living in one alone.

BEN: There's certainly no law requiring you to do that. Is this . . . Bruce someone you're seeing?

NED: Why thank you for asking. Don't I wish. I see him. He just doesn't see me. Everyone's afraid of me anyway. I frighten them away. It's called the lemon complex.

BEN: I think you're the one who's scared.

NED: You've never said that before.

BEN: Yes, I have. You just didn't hear me. What's the worst thing that could happen to you.

NED: I'd spend a million bucks on a house. Look, Ben—please! (*He takes the blueprints from him.*) I've—we've started an organization to raise money and spread information and fight any way we can.

BEN: Fight who and what?

NED: I told you. There's this strange new disease . . .

BEN: You're not going to do that full-time?

NED: I just want to help it get started and I'll worry about how much time later on.

BEN: It sounds to me like another excuse to keep from writing.

NED: I knew you would say that. I was wondering . . . could your law firm incorporate us and get us tax-exempt status and take us on for free, what's it called, *pro bono?*

BEN: *Pro bono* for what? What are you going to do?

NED: I just told you—raise money and fight.

BEN: You have to be more specific than that. You have to have a plan.

NED: How about if we say we're going to become a cross between the League of Women Voters and the United States Marines? Is that a good-enough plan?

BEN: Well, we have a committee that decides this sort of thing. I'll have to put it to the committee.

NED: Why can't you just say yes?

BEN: Because we have a committee.

NED: But you're the senior partner and I'm your brother.

BEN: I fail to see what bearing that has on the matter. You're asking me to ask my partners to give up income that would ordinarily come into their pocket.

NED: I thought every law firm did a certain amount of this sort of thing—charity, worthy causes.

BEN: It's not up to me, however, to select just what these worthy causes might be.

NED: Well, that's a pity. What did you start the firm for?

BEN: That's one of our rules. It's a democratic firm.

NED: I think I like elitism better. When will you know?

BEN: Know what?

NED: Whether or not your committee wants to help dying faggots?

BEN: I'll put it to them at the next meeting.

NED: When is that?

BEN: When it is!

NED: When is it? Because if you're not going to help, I have to find somebody else.

BEN: You're more than free to do that.

NED: I don't want to do that! I want my big brother's fancy famous big-deal straight law firm to be the first major New York law firm to do *pro bono* work for a gay cause. That would give me a great deal of pride. I'm sorry you can't see that. I'm sorry I'm still putting you in a position where you're ashamed of me. I thought we'd worked all that out years ago.

BEN: I am not ashamed of you! I told you I'm simply not free to take this on without asking my partners' approval at the next meeting.

NED: Why don't I believe that. When is the next meeting?

BEN: Next Monday. Can you wait until next Monday?

NED: Who else is on the committee?

BEN: What difference does that make?

NED: I'll lobby them. You don't seem like a very sure vote. Is Nelson on the committee? Norman Ivey? Harvey?

BEN: Norman and Harvey are.

NED: Good.

BEN: Okay? Lemon, where do you want to have lunch today? It's your turn to pay.

NED: It is not. I paid last week.

BEN: That's simply not true.

NED: Last week was . . . French. You're right. Do you know you're the only person in the world I can't get mad at and stay mad at. I think my world would come to an end without you. And then who would Ben talk to? (*He embraces* BEN.)

BEN: (*Embracing back, a bit.*) That's true.

NED: You're getting better at it.

Scene 4

NED's *apartment. It is stark, modern, all black and white.* FELIX *comes walking in from another room with a beer, and* NED *follows, carrying one, too.*

FELIX: That's quite a library in there. You read all those books?

NED: Why does everybody ask that?

FELIX: You have a whole room of 'em, you must want to get asked.

NED: I never thought of it that way. Maybe I do. Thank you. But no, of course I haven't. They go out of print and then you can't find them, so I buy them right away.

FELIX: I think you're going to have to face the fact you won't be able to read them all before you die.

NED: I think you're right.

FELIX: You know, I really used to like high tech, hut I'm tired of it now. I think I want chintz back again. Don't be insulted.

NED: I'm not. I want chintz back again, too.

FELIX: So here we are—two fellows who want chintz back again. Excuse me for saying so, but you are stiff as starch.

NED: It's been a long time since I've had a date. This is a date, isn't it? (FELIX *nods.*) And on the rare occasion, I was usually the asker.

FELIX: That's what's thrown you off your style: I called and asked.

NED: Some style. Before any second date I usually receive a phone call that starts with "Now I don't know what you had in mind, but can't we just be friends?"

FELIX: No. Are you glad I'm here?

NED: Oh, I'm pleased as punch you're here. You're very good-looking. What are you doing here?

FELIX: I'll let that tiny bit of self-pity pass for the moment.

NED: It's not self-pity, it's nervousness.

FELIX: It's definitely self-pity. Do you think you're bad-looking?

NED: Where are you from?

FELIX: I'm from Oklahoma. I left home at eighteen and put myself through college. My folks are dead. My dad worked at the refinery in West Tulsa and my mom was a waitress at a luncheonette in Walgreen's.

NED: Isn't it amazing how a kid can come out of all that and wind up on the *Times* dictating taste and style and fashion to the entire world?

FELIX: And we were talking so nicely.

NED: Talking is not my problem. Shutting up is my problem. And keeping my hands off you.

FELIX: You don't have to keep your hands off me. You have very nice hands. Do you have any awkward sexual tendencies you want to tell me about, too? That I'm not already familiar with?

NED: What are you familiar with?

FELIX: I have found myself pursuing men who hurt me. Before minor therapy. You're not one of those?

NED: No, I'm the runner. I *was* the runner. Until major therapy. After people who didn't want me and away from people who do.

FELIX: Isn't it amazing how a kid can come out of all that analyzing everything incessantly down to the most infinitesimal neurosis and still be all alone?

NED: I'm sorry you don't like my Dr. Freud. Another aging Jew who couldn't get laid.

FELIX: Just relax. You'll get laid.

NED: I try being laid-back, assertive, funny, butch . . . What's the point? I don't think there are many gay relationships that work out anyway.

FELIX: It's difficult to imagine you being laid-back. I know a lot of gay relationships that are working out very well.

NED: I guess I never see them.

FELIX: That's because you're a basket case.

NED: Fuck off.

FELIX: What's the matter? Don't you think you're attractive? Don't you like your body?

NED: I don't think anybody really likes their body. I read that somewhere.

FELIX: You know my fantasy has always been to go away and live by the ocean and write twenty-four novels, living with someone just like you with all these books who of course will be right there beside me writing your own twenty-four novels.

NED: (*After a beat.*) Me, too.

FELIX: Harold Robbins marries James Michener.

NED: How about Tolstoy and Charles Dickens?

FELIX: As long as Kafka doesn't marry Dostoevsky.

NED: Dostoevsky is my favorite writer.

FELIX: I'll have to try him again.

NED: If you really feel that way, why do you write all that society and party and fancy-ball-gown bullshit?

FELIX: Here we go again. I'll bet you gobble it up every day.

NED: I do. I also know six people who've died. When I came to you a few weeks ago, it was only one.

FELIX: I'm sorry. Is that why you agreed to this date?

NED: Do you know that when Hitler's Final Solution to eliminate the Polish Jews was first mentioned in the *Times* it was on page twenty-eight. And on page six of the *Washington Post.* And the *Times* and the *Post* were owned by Jews. What causes silence like that? Why didn't the American Jews help the German Jews get out? Their very own people! Scholars are finally writing honestly about this—I've been doing some research—and it's damning to everyone who was here then: Jewish leadership for being totally ineffective; Jewish organizations for constantly fighting among themselves, unable to cooperate even in the face of death: Zionists versus non-Zionists, Rabbi Wise against Rabbi Silver ...

FELIX: Is this some sort of special way you talk when you don't want to talk? We were doing so nicely.

NED: We were?

FELIX: Wasn't there an awful lot of anti-Semitism in those days? Weren't Jews afraid of rubbing people's noses in too much shit?

NED: Yes, everybody has a million excuses for not getting involved. But aren't there moral obligations, moral commandments to try everything possible? Where were the Christian churches, the Pope, Churchill? And don't get me started on Roosevelt ... How I was brought up to worship him, all Jews were. A clear statement from him would have put everything on the front pages, would have put Hitler on notice. But his administration did its best to stifle publicity at the same time as they clamped down immigration laws forbidding entry, and this famous haven for the oppressed became as inaccessible as Tibet. The title of Treasury Secretary Morgenthau's report to Roosevelt was "Acquiescence of This Government in the Murder of the Jews," which he wrote in 1944. Dachau was opened in 1933. Where was everybody for eleven years? And then it was too late.

FELIX: This is turning out to be a very romantic evening.

NED: And don't tell me how much you can accomplish working from the inside. Jewish leaders, relying on their contacts with people in high places, were still, quietly, from the inside, attempting to persuade them when the war was over.

FELIX: What do you want me to say? Do you ever take a vacation?

NED: A vacation. I forgot. That's the great goal, isn't it. A constant Fire Island vacation. Party, party; fuck, fuck. Maybe you can give me a few trendy pointers on what to wear.

FELIX: Boy, you really have a bug up your ass. Look, I'm not going to tell them I'm gay and could I write about the few cases of a mysterious disease that seems to be standing in the way of your kissing me even though there must be half a million gay men in this city who are fine and healthy. Let us please acknowledge the law of averages. And this is not World War Two. The numbers are nowhere remotely comparable. And all analogies to the Holocaust are tired, overworked, boring, probably insulting, possibly true, and a major turnoff.

NED: Are they?

FELIX: Boy, I think I've found myself a real live weird one. I had no idea. (*Pause.*) Hey, I just called you weird.

NED: You are not the first.

FELIX: You've never had a lover, have you?

NED: Where did you get that from?

FELIX: Have you? Wow.

NED: I suppose you've had quite a few.

FELIX: I had a very good one for a number of years, thank you. He was older than I was and he found someone younger.

NED: So you like them older. You looking for a father?

FELIX: No, I am not looking for a father! God, you are relentless. And as cheery as Typhoid Mary.

(NED *comes over to* FELIX *and sits beside him. Then he leans over and kisses him. The kiss becomes quite intense. Then* NED *breaks away, jumps up, and begins to walk around nervously.*)

NED: The American Jews knew exactly what was happening, but everything was downplayed and stifled. Can you imagine how effective it would have been if every Jew in America had marched on Washington? Proudly! Who says I want a lover? Huh!? I mean, why doesn't anybody believe me when I say I do not want a lover?

FELIX: You are fucking crazy. Jews, Dachau, Final Solution—what kind of date is this! I don't believe anyone in the whole wide world doesn't want to be loved. Ned, you don't remember me, do you? We've been in bed together. We made love. We talked. We kissed. We cuddled. We made love again. I keep waiting for you to remember, something, anything. But you don't!

NED: How could I not remember you?

FELIX: I don't know.

NED: Maybe if I saw you naked.

FELIX: It's okay as long as we treat each other like whores. It was at the baths a few years ago. You were busy cruising some blond number and I stood outside your door waiting for you to come back and when you did you gave me such an inspection up and down you would have thought I was applying for the CIA.

NED: And then what?

FELIX: I just told you. We made love twice. I thought it was lovely. You told me your name was Ned, that when you were a child you read a Philip Barry play called *Holiday* where there was a

Ned, and you immediately switched from ... Alexander? I teased you for taking such a Wasp, up-in-Connecticut-for-the-weekend name, and I asked what you did, and you answered something like you'd tried a number of things, and I asked you if that had included love, which is when you said you had to get up early in the morning. That's when I left. But I tossed you my favorite go-fuck-yourself when you told me "I really am not in the market for a lover"—men do not just naturally not love—they learn not to. I am not a whore. I just sometimes make mistakes and look for love in the wrong places. And I think you're a bluffer. Your novel was all about a man desperate for love and a relationship, in a world filled with nothing but casual sex.

NED: Do you think we could start over?

FELIX: Maybe.

Scene 5

NED's *apartment.* MICKEY, BRUCE, *and* TOMMY BOATWRIGHT, *a Southerner in his late twenties, are stuffing envelopes with various inserts and then packing them into cartons. Beer and pretzels.*

MICKEY: (*Calling off.*) Ned, Gregory says hello and he can't believe you've turned into an activist. He says where were you fifteen years ago when we needed you.

NED: (*Coming in with a tray with more beer.*) You tell Gregory fifteen years ago no self-respecting faggot would have anything to do with you guys.

TOMMY: I was twelve years old.

BRUCE: We're not activists.

MICKEY: If you're not an activist, Bruce, then what are you?

BRUCE: Nothing. I'm only in this until it goes away.

MICKEY: You know, the battle against the police at Stonewall was won by transvestites. We all fought like hell. It's you Brooks Brothers guys who—

BRUCE: That's why I wasn't at Stonewall. I don't have anything in common with those guys, girls, whatever you call them. Ned, Robert Stokes has it. He called me today.

NED: At Glenn Fitzsimmons' party the other night, I saw one friend there I knew was sick, I learned about two others, and then walking home I bumped into Richie Faro, who told me he'd just been diagnosed.

MICKEY: Richie Faro?

NED: All this on Sixth Avenue between Nineteenth and Eighth Streets.

MICKEY: Richie Faro—gee, I haven't seen him since Stonewall. I think we even had a little affairlet.

BRUCE: Are you a transvestite?

MICKEY: No, but I'll fight for your right to be one.

BRUCE: I don't want to be one!

MICKEY: I'm worried this organization might only attract white bread and middle-class. We need blacks ...

TOMMY: Right on!

MICKEY: ... and ... how do you feel about lesbians?

BRUCE: Not very much. I mean, they're ... something else.

MICKEY: I wonder what they're going to think about all this. If past history is any guide, there's never been much support by either half of us for the other. Tommy, are you a lesbian?

TOMMY: (*As he exits into the kitchen.*) I have done and seen everything.

NED: (*To* BRUCE) How are you doing?

BRUCE: I'm okay now. I forgot to thank you for sending flowers.

NED: That's okay.

BRUCE: Funny—my mother sent flowers. We've never even talked about my being gay. I told her Craig died. I guess she knew.

NED: I think mothers somehow always know. Would you like to have dinner next week, maybe see a movie?

BRUCE: (*Uncomfortable when* NED *makes advances.*) Actually ... it's funny ... it happened so fast. You know Albert? I've been seeing him.

NED: That guy in the Calvin Klein ads? Great!

(TOMMY *returns dragging another carton of envelopes and boxes.*)

BRUCE: I don't think I like to be alone. I've always been with somebody.

MICKEY: (*Looking up from his list-checking.*) We have to choose a president tonight, don't forget. I'm not interested. And what about a board of directors?

BRUCE: (*Looking at one of the flyers.*) Mickey, how did you finally decide to say it? I didn't even look.

MICKEY: I just said the best medical knowledge, which admittedly isn't very much, seems to feel that a virus has landed in our community. It could have been any community, but it landed in ours. I guess we just got in the way. Boy, are we going to have paranoia problems.

NED: (*Looking at a flyer.*) That's all you said?

MICKEY: See what I mean? No, I also put in the benefit dance announcement and a coupon for donations.

NED: What about the recommendations?

MICKEY: I recommend everyone should donate a million dollars. How are we going to make people realize this is not just a gay problem? If it happens to us, it can happen to anybody. I sent copies to all the gay newspapers.

BRUCE: What good will that do? Nobody reads them.

MICKEY: The *Native*'s doing a good job.

NED: (*Who has read the flyer and is angry.*) Mickey, I thought we talked this out on the phone. We must tell everybody what Emma wants us to tell them.

MICKEY: She wants to tell them so badly she won't lend her name as recommending it. (*To the others.*) This is what Ned wrote for me to send out. "If this doesn't scare the shit out of you, and rouse you to action, gay men may have no future here on earth." Neddie, I think that's a bit much.

BRUCE: You'll scare everybody to death!

NED: Shake up. What's wrong with that? This isn't something that can be force-fed gently; it won't work. Mickey neglected to read my first sentence.

MICKEY: "It's difficult to write this without sounding alarmist or scared." Okay, but then listen to this: "I am sick of guys moaning that giving up careless sex until this blows over is worse than death . . . I am sick of guys who can only think with their cocks . . . I am sick of closeted gays. It's 1982 now, guys, when are you going to come out? By 1984 you could be dead."

BRUCE: You're crazy.

NED: Am I? There are almost five hundred cases now. Okay, if we're not sending it out, I'll get the *Native* to run it.

BRUCE: But we can't tell people how to live their lives! We can't do that. And besides, the entire gay political platform is fucking. We'd get it from all sides.

NED: You make it sound like that's all that being gay means.

BRUCE: That's all it does mean!

MICKEY: It's the only thing that makes us different.

NED: I don't want to be considered different.

BRUCE: Neither do I, actually.

MICKEY: Well, I do.

BRUCE: Well, you are!

NED: Why is it we can only talk about our sexuality, and so relentlessly? You know, Mickey, all we've created is generations of guys who can't deal with each other as anything but erections. We can't even get a meeting with the mayor's gay assistant!

TOMMY: I'm very interested in setting up some sort of services for the patients. We've got to start thinking about them.

BRUCE: (*Whispering to* NED.) Who's he?

TOMMY: He heard about you and he found you and here he is. My name is Tommy Boatwright... (*To* NED.) Why don't you write that down? Tommy Boatwright. In real life, I'm a hospital administrator. And I'm a Southern bitch.

NED: Welcome to gay politics.

BRUCE: Ned, I won't have anything to do with any organization that tells people how to live their lives.

NED: It's not telling them. It's a recommendation.

MICKEY: With a shotgun to their heads.

BRUCE: It's interfering with their civil rights.

MICKEY: Fucking as a civil right? Don't we just wish.

TOMMY: What if we put it in the form of a recommendation from gay doctors? So that way we're just the conduit.

NED: I can't get any gay doctor to go on record and say publicly what Emma wants.

BRUCE: The fortunes they've made off our being sick, you'd think they could have warned us. (*Suddenly noticing an envelope.*) What the fuck is this?

MICKEY: Unh, oh!

BRUCE: Look at this! Was this your idea?

NED: I'm looking. I'm not seeing. What don't I see?

MICKEY: What we put for our return address.

NED: You mean the word "gay" is on the envelope?

BRUCE: You're damn right. Instead of just the initials. Who did it?

NED: Well, maybe it was Pierre who designed it. Maybe it was a mistake at the printers. But it is the name we chose for this organization . . .

BRUCE: You chose. I didn't want "gay" in it.

MICKEY: No, we all voted. That was one of those meetings when somebody actually showed up.

NED: Bruce, I think it's interesting that nobody noticed until now. You've been stuffing them all week at your apartment.

BRUCE: We can't send them out.

NED: We have to if we want anybody to come to the dance. They were late from the printers as it is.

BRUCE: We can go through and scratch out the word with a Magic Marker.

NED: Ten thousand times? Look, I feel sympathy for young guys still living at home on Long Island with their parents, but most men getting these . . . Look at you, in your case what difference does it make? You live alone, you own your own apartment, your mother lives in another state . . .

BRUCE: What about my mailman?

(MICKEY *lets out a little laughing yelp, then clears his throat.*)

NED: You don't expect me to take that seriously?

BRUCE: Yes, I do!

NED: What about your doorman?

BRUCE: What about him?

NED: Why don't you worry about him? All those cute little Calvin Klein numbers you parade under his nose, he thinks you're playing poker with the boys?

BRUCE: You don't have any respect for anyone who doesn't think like you do, do you?

NED: Bruce, I don't agree with you about this. I think it's imperative that we all grow up now and come out of the closet.

MICKEY: Ladies, behave! Ned, you don't think much of our sexual revolution. You say it all the time.

NED: No, I say I don't think much of promiscuity. And what's that got to do with gay envelopes?

MICKEY: But you've certainly done your share.

NED: That doesn't mean I approve of it or like myself for doing it.

MICKEY: But not all of us feel that way. And we don't like to hear the word "promiscuous" used pejoratively.

BRUCE: Or so publicly.

NED: Where the world can hear it, Bruce?

MICKEY: Sex is liberating. It's always guys like you who've never had one who are always screaming about relationships, and monogamy and fidelity and holy matrimony. What are you, a closet straight?

NED: Mickey, more sex isn't more liberating. And having so much sex makes finding love impossible.

MICKEY: Neddie, dahling, do not put your failure to find somebody on the morality of all the rest of us.

NED: Mickey, dahling, I'm just saying what I think! It's taken me twenty years of assorted forms of therapy in various major world capitals to be able to do so without guilt, fear, or giving a fuck if anybody likes it or not.

TOMMY: I'll buy that!

NED: Thank you.

BRUCE: But not everyone's so free to say what they think!

MICKEY: Or able to afford so much therapy. Although God knows I need it. (*Looking at his watch.*) Look, it's late, and we haven't elected our president. Ned, I think it should be ... Bruce. Everybody knows him and likes him and ... I mean, everybody expects you to—

NED: You mean he's popular and everybody's afraid of me.

MICKEY: Yes.

TOMMY: No.

MICKEY: No.

TOMMY: No, what it means is that you have a certain kind of energy that's definitely needed, but Bruce has a . . . presence that might bring people together in a way you can't.

NED: What's that mean?

TOMMY: It means he's gorgeous—and all the kids on Christopher Street and Fire Island will feel a bit more comfortable following him.

NED: Just like high school.

TOMMY and MICKEY: Yes!

NED: Follow him where?

TOMMY: (*Putting his arm around him.*) Well, honey, why don't we have a little dinner and I'll tell you all about it—and more.

NED: Unh, thanks, I'm busy.

TOMMY: Forever? Well, that's too bad. I wanted to try my hand at smoothing out your rough edges.

MICKEY: Good luck.

NED: (*To* BRUCE.) Well, it looks like you're the president.

BRUCE: I don't think I want this.

NED: Oh, come on, you're gorgeous—and we're all going to follow you.

BRUCE: Fuck you. I accept.

NED: Well, fuck you, congratulations.

TOMMY: There are going to be a lot of scared people out there needing someplace to call for information. I'd be interested in starting some sort of telephone hot line.

BRUCE: (*His first decision in office.*) Unh . . . sure. Just prepare a detailed budget and let me see it before you make any commitments.

MICKEY: (*To* NED.) Don't you feel in safe hands already?

TOMMY: (*To* BRUCE.) What is it you do for a living, if I may ask?

BRUCE: I'm a vice-president of Citibank.

TOMMY: That's nothing to be shy about, sugar. You invented the Cash Machine. (*Picking up an envelope.*) So, are we mailing these out or what?

BRUCE: What do you think?

TOMMY: I'll bet nobody even notices.

BRUCE: Oh, there will be some who notice. Okay.

TOMMY: Okay? Okay! Our first adult compromise. Thank y'all for your cooperation.

(FELIX, *carrying a shopping bag, lets himself in with his own key.* NED *goes to greet him.*)

NED: Everybody, this is Felix. Bruce, Tommy, Mickey. Bruce just got elected president.

FELIX: My condolences. Don't let me interrupt. Anybody want any Balducci gourmet ice cream—it's eighteen bucks a pint?

(NED *and* FELIX *go into the kitchen.*)

MICKEY: It looks like Neddie's found a boyfriend.

BRUCE: Thank God, now maybe he'll leave me alone.

TOMMY: Shit, he's got his own key. It looks like I signed on too late.

BRUCE: I worry about Ned. I mean, I like him a lot, but his style is so . . . confrontational. We could get into a lot of trouble with him.

TOMMY: Honey, he looks like a pretty good catch to me. We could get into a lot of trouble without him.

(NED *and* FELIX *come back.* FELIX *cleans up after the guys.*)

MICKEY: I'm going home. My Gregory, he burns dinner every night, and when I'm late, he blames me.

BRUCE: (*To* NED.) My boss doesn't know and he hates gays. He keeps telling me fag jokes and I keep laughing at them.

NED: Citibank won't fire you for being gay. And if they did, we could make such a stink that every gay customer in New York would leave them. Come on, Bruce—you used to be a fucking Green Beret!

TOMMY: Goodness!

BRUCE: But I love my job. I supervise a couple thousand people all over the country and the investments I look after are up to twenty million now.

MICKEY: I'm leaving. (*He hefts a carton and starts out.*)

BRUCE: Wait, I'm coming. (*To* NED.) I just think we have to stay out of anything political.

(FELIX *goes back into the kitchen.*)

NED: And I think it's going to be impossible to pass along *any* information or recommendation that isn't going to be considered political by somebody.

TOMMY: And I think this is not an argument you two boys are going to settle tonight.

(BRUCE *starts out and as he passes* NED, NED *stops him and kisses him good-bye on the mouth.* BRUCE *picks up a big carton and heads out.*)

TOMMY: (*Who has waited impatiently for Bruce to leave so he can be alone with Ned.*) I just wanted to tell you I really admire your writing . . . and your passion . . . (*As* FELIX *reenters from the kitchen,* TOMMY *drops his flirtatious tone.*) . . . and what you've been saying and doing, and it's because of you I'm here. (*To* FELIX.) Take care this good man doesn't burn out. Good night. (*He leaves.*)

NED: We just elected a president who's in the closet. I lost every argument. And I'm the only screamer among them. Oh, I forgot to tell them—I'm getting us something on the local news.

FELIX: Which channel?

NED: It's not TV, it's radio . . . It's a start.

FELIX: Ned, I think you should have been president.

NED: I didn't really want it. I've never been any good playing on a team. I like stirring things up on my own. Bruce will be a good president. I'll shape him up. Where's the ice cream? Do you think I'm crazy?

FELIX: I certainly do. That's why I'm here.

NED: I'm so glad.

FELIX: That I'm here?

NED: That you think I'm crazy. (*They kiss.*)

Scene 6

BEN's *office. In a corner is a large model of the new house under a cloth cover.*

BEN: You got your free legal work from my firm; now I'm not going to be on your board of directors, too.

NED: I got our free legal work from your firm by going to Norman and he said, "Of course, no problem." I asked him, "Don't you have to put it before your committee?" And he said, "Nah, I'll just tell them we're going to do it."

BEN: Well . . . you got it.

NED: All I'm asking for is the use of your name. You don't have to do a thing. This is an honorary board. For the stationery.

BEN: Ned, come on—it's your cause, not mine.

NED: That is just an evasion!

BEN: It is not. I don't ask you to help me with the Larchmont school board, do I?

NED: But I would if you asked me.

BEN: But I don't.

NED: Would you be more interested if you thought this was a straight disease?

BEN: It has nothing to do with your being gay.

NED: Of course it has. What else has it got to do with?

BEN: I've got other things to do.

NED: But I'm telling you you don't have to do a thing!

BEN: The answer is No.

NED: It's impossible to get this epidemic taken seriously. I wrote a letter to the gay newspaper and some guy wrote in, "Oh there goes Ned Weeks again; he wants us all to die so he can say 'I told you so.'"

BEN: He sounds like a crazy.

NED: It kept me up all night.

BEN: Then you're crazy, too.

NED: I ran into an old friend I hadn't seen in years in the subway, and I said, "Hello, how are you?" He started screaming, "You're giving away all our secrets, you're painting us as sick, you're destroying homosexuality"—and then he tried to slug me. Right there in the subway. Under Bloomingdale's.

BEN: Another crazy.

NED: We did raise $50,000 at our dance last week. That's more money than any gay organization has ever raised at one time in this city before.

BEN: That's wonderful, Ned. So you must be beginning to do something right.

NED: And I made a speech appealing for volunteers and we got over a hundred people to sign up, including a few women. And I've got us on Donahue. I'm going to be on national TV with a doctor and a patient.

BEN: Don't tell your mother.

NED: Why not?

BEN: She's afraid someone is going to shoot you.

(BEN *rolls the model house stage center and pulls off the cover.*)

NED: What about you? Aren't you afraid your corporate clients will say, "Was that your faggot brother I saw on TV?" Excuse me—is this a bad time? You seem preoccupied.

BEN: Do I? I'm sorry. A morning with the architect is enough to shake me up a little bit. It's going to cost more than I thought.

NED: More?

BEN: Twice as much.

NED: Two million?

BEN: I can handle it.

NED: You can? That's very nice. You know, Ben, one of these days I'll make you agree that over twenty million men and women are not all here on this earth because of something requiring the services of a psychiatrist.

BEN: Oh, it's up to twenty million now, is it? Every time we have this discussion, you up the ante.

NED: We haven't had this discussion in years, Ben. And we grow, just like everybody else.

BEN: Look, I try to understand. I read stuff. (*Picking up a copy of* Newsweek, *with "Gay America" on the cover.*) I open magazines and I see pictures of you guys in leather and chains and whips and black masks, with captions saying this is a social worker, this is a computer analyst, this is a schoolteacher—and I say to myself, "This isn't Ned."

NED: No, it isn't. It isn't most of us. You know the media always dramatizes the most extreme. Do you think we all wear dresses, too?

BEN: Don't you?

NED: Me, personally? No, I do not.

BEN: But then you tell me how you go to the bathhouses and fuck blindly, and to me that's not so different from this. You guys don't seem to understand why there are rules, and regulations, guidelines, responsibilities. You guys have a dreadful image problem.

NED: I know that! That's what has to be changed. That's why it's so important to have people like you supporting us. You're a respected person. You already have your dignity.

BEN: We better decide where we're going to eat lunch and get out of here. I have an important meeting.

NED: Do you? How important? I've asked for your support.

BEN: In every area I consider important you have my support.

NED: In some place deep inside of you you still think I'm sick. Isn't that right? Okay. Define it for me. What do you mean by "sick"? Sick unhealthy? Sick perverted? Sick I'll get over it? Sick to be locked up?

BEN: I think you've adjusted to life quite well.

NED: All things considered? (BEN *nods*.) In the only area I consider important I don't have your support at all. The single-minded determination of all you people to forever see us as sick helps keep us sick.

BEN: I saw how unhappy you were!

NED: So were you! You wound up going to shrinks, too. We grew up side by side. We both felt pretty much the same about Mom and Pop. I refuse to accept for one more second that I was damaged by our childhood while you were not.

BEN: But we all don't react the same way to the same thing.

NED: That's right. So I became a writer and you became a lawyer. I'll agree to the fact that I have any number of awful character traits. But not to the fact that whatever they did to us as kids automatically made me sick and gay while you stayed straight and healthy.

BEN: Well, that's the difference of opinion we have over theory.

NED: But your theory turns me into a man from Mars. My theory doesn't do that to you.

BEN: Are you suggesting it was wrong of me to send you into therapy so young? I didn't think you'd stay in it forever.

NED: I didn't think I'd done anything wrong until you sent me into it. Ben, you know you mean more to me than anyone else in the world; you always have. Although I think I've finally found someone I like . . . Don't you understand?

BEN: No, I don't understand.

NED: You've got to say it. I'm the same as you. Just say it. Say it!

BEN: No, you're not. I can't say it.

NED: (*He is heartbroken.*) Every time I lose this fight it hurts more. I don't want to have lunch. I'll see you. (*He starts out.*)

BEN: Come on, Lemon, I still love you. Sarah loves you. Our children. Our cat. Our dog . . .

NED: You think this is a joke!

BEN: (*Angry.*) You have my love and you have my legal advice and my financial supervision. I can't give you the courage to stand up and say to me that you don't give a good healthy fuck what I think. Please stop trying to wring some admission of guilt out of me. I am truly happy that you've met someone. It's about time. And I'm sorry your friends are dying . . .

NED: If you're so sorry, join our honorary board and say you're sorry out loud!

BEN: My agreeing you were born just like I was born is not going to help save your dying friends.

NED: Funny—that's exactly what I think will help save my dying friends.

BEN: Ned—you can be gay and you can be proud no matter what I think. Everybody is oppressed by somebody else in some form or another. Some of us learn how to fight back, with or without the help of others, despite their opinions, even those closest to us. And judging from this mess your friends are in, it's imperative that you stand up and fight to be prouder than ever.

NED: Can't you see that I'm trying to do that? Can't your perverse ego proclaiming its superiority see that I'm trying to be proud? You can only find room to call yourself normal.

BEN: You make me sound like I'm the enemy.

NED: I'm beginning to think that you and your straight world are our enemy. I am furious with you, and with myself and with every goddamned doctor who ever told me I'm sick and interfered with my loving a man. I'm trying to understand why nobody wants to hear we're dying, why nobody wants to help, why my own brother doesn't want to help. Two million dollars—for a house! We can't even get twenty-nine cents from the city. You still think I'm sick, and I simply cannot allow that any longer. I will not speak to you again until you accept me as your equal. Your healthy equal. Your brother! (*He runs out.*)

Scene 7

NED's *apartment.* FELIX, *working on an article, is spread out on the floor with books, note pad, comforter, and pillows.* NED *enters, eating from a pint of ice cream.*

NED: At the rate I'm going, no one in this city will be talking to me in about three more weeks. I had another fight with Bruce today. I slammed the phone down on him. I don't know why I do that—I'm never finished saying what I want to, so I just have to call him back, during which I inevitably work myself up into another frenzy and hang up on him again. That poor man doesn't know what to do with me. I don't think people like me work at Citibank.

FELIX: Why can't you see what an ordinary guy Bruce is? I know you think he has hidden qualities, if you just give him plant food he'll grow into the fighter you are. He can't. All he's got is a lot of good-looking Pendleton shirts.

NED: I know there are better ways to handle him. I just can't seem to. This epidemic is killing friendships, too. I can't even talk to my own brother. Why doesn't he call me?

FELIX: There's the phone.

NED: Why do I always have to do the running back?

FELIX: All you ever eat is desserts.

NED: Sugar is the most important thing in my life. All the rest is just to stay alive.

FELIX: What was the fight about?

NED: Which fight?

FELIX: Bruce.

NED: Pick a subject.

FELIX: How many do you know now?

NED: Forty . . . dead. That's too many for one person to know. Curt Morgan, this guy I went to Yale with, just died.

FELIX: Emerick Nolan—he gave me my first job on the *Washington Post*.

NED: Bruce is getting paranoid: now his lover, Albert, isn't feeling well. Bruce is afraid he's giving it to everyone.

FELIX: Maybe it isn't paranoia. Maybe what we do with our lovers is what we should be thinking about most of all.

(*The phone rings.* NED *answers it.*)

NED: Hello. Hold on. (*Locating some pages and reading from them into the phone.*) "It is no secret that I consider the mayor to be, along with the *Times*, the biggest enemy gay men and women must contend with in New York. Until the day I die I will never forgive this newspaper and this mayor for ignoring this epidemic that is killing so many of my friends. If . . ." All right, here's the end. "And every gay man who refuses to come forward now and fight to save his own life is truly helping to kill the rest of us. How many of us have to die before you get scared off your ass and into action?" . . . Thank *you*. (*He hangs up.*) I hear it's becoming known as the Ned Weeks School of Outrage.

FELIX: Who was that?

NED: Felix, I'm orchestrating this really well. I know I am. We have over six hundred volunteers now. I've got us mentioned in *Time, Newsweek*, the evening news on all three networks, both local and national, English and French and Canadian and Australian TV, all the New York area papers except the *Times* and the *Voice* . . .

FELIX: You're doing great.

NED: But they don't support me! Bruce . . . this fucking board of directors we put together, all friends of mine—every single one of them yelled at me for two solid hours last night. They think I'm creating a panic, I'm using it to make myself into a celebrity—not one of them will appear on TV or be interviewed, so I do it all by default; so now I'm accused of being self-serving, as if it's fun getting slugged on the subway.

FELIX: They're beginning to get really frightened. You are becoming a leader. And you love to fight.

NED: What? I love it?

FELIX: Yes!

NED: I love to fight? *Moi?*

FELIX: Yes, you do, and you're having a wonderful time.

NED: Yes, I am. (*Meaning* FELIX.)

FELIX: I did speak to one of our science reporters today.

NED: (*Delighted.*) Felix! What did he say?

FELIX: He's gay, too, and afraid they'll find out. Don't yell at me! Ned, I tried. All those shrinks, they must have done something right to you.

NED: (*Giving* FELIX *a kiss with each name.*) Dr. Malev, Dr. Ritvo, Dr. Gillespie, Dr. Greenacre, Dr. Harkavy, Dr. Klagsbrun, Dr. Donadello, Dr. Levy ... I have only one question now: why did it have to take so long?

FELIX: You think it's them, do you?

NED: Dr.—I can't remember which one—said it would finally happen. Someone I couldn't scare away would finally show up.

FELIX: At the baths, why didn't you tell me you were a writer?

NED: Why didn't you tell me you worked for the *Times?* That I would have remembered.

FELIX: If I had told you what I did, would you have seen me again?

NED: Absolutely.

FELIX: You slut!

NED: Felix, we weren't ready then. If I had it, would you leave me?

FELIX: I don't know. Would you, if I did?

NED: No.

FELIX: How do you know?

NED: I just know. You had to have had my mother. She was a dedicated full-time social worker for the Red Cross—she put me to work on the Bloodmobile when I was eight. She was always getting an award for being best bloodcatcher or something. She's eighty now—touring China. I don't think I'm programmed any other way.

FELIX: I have something to tell you.

NED: You're pregnant.

FELIX: I was married once.

NED: Does that make me the other woman?

FELIX: I thought I was supposed to be straight. She said I had been unfair to her, which I had been. I have a son.

NED: You have a son?

FELIX: She won't let me see him.

NED: You can't see your own son? But didn't you fight? That means you're ashamed. So he will be, too.

FELIX: That's why I didn't tell you before. And who says I didn't fight! What happens to someone who cannot be as strong as you want them to be?

NED: Felix, weakness terrifies me. It scares the shit out of me. My father was weak and I'm afraid I'll be like him. His life didn't stand for anything, and then it was over. So I fight. Constantly. And if I can do it, I can't understand why everybody else can't do it, too. Okay?

FELIX: Okay. (*He pulls off one of his socks and shows* NED *a purple spot on his foot.*) It keeps getting bigger and bigger, Neddie, and it doesn't go away.

End of Act One

Act Two

Scene 8

EMMA's *apartment.* EMMA *and* NED *are having brunch. She uses a non-motorized, i.e., regular, wheelchair.*

NED: You look very pretty.

EMMA: Thank you.

NED: Where's your cat?

EMMA: Under my bed. She's afraid of you.

NED: Do you think being Jewish makes you always hungry?

EMMA: I'm not Jewish.

NED: You're not?

EMMA: I'm German.

NED: Everyone thinks you're Jewish.

EMMA: I know. In medicine that helps.

NED: How many of us do you think already have the virus in our system?

EMMA: In this city—easily over half of all gay men.

NED: So we're just walking time bombs—waiting for whatever it is that sets us off.

EMMA: Yes. And before a vaccine can be discovered almost every gay man will have been exposed. Ned, your organization is worthless! I went up and down Christopher Street last night and all I saw was guys going in the bars alone and coming out with somebody. And outside the baths, all I saw was lines of guys going in. And what is this stupid publication you finally put out? (*She holds up a pamphlet.*) After all we've talked about? You leave too much margin for intelligence. Why aren't you telling them, bluntly, stop! Every day you don't tell them, more people infect each other.

NED: Don't lecture me. I'm on your side. Remember?

EMMA: Don't be on my side! I don't need you on my side. Make your side shape up. I've seen 238 cases—me: one doctor. You make it sound like there's nothing worse going around than measles.

NED: They wouldn't print what I wrote. Again.

EMMA: What do you mean "they"? Who's they? I thought you and Bruce were the leaders.

NED: Now we've got a board. You need a board of directors when you become tax-exempt. It was a pain in the ass finding anyone to serve on it at all! I called every prominent gay man I could get to. Forget it! Finally, what we put together turns out to be a bunch as timid as Bruce. And every time Bruce doesn't agree with me, he puts it to a board vote.

EMMA: And you lose.

NED: (*Nods.*) Bruce is in the closet; Mickey works for the Health

Department; he starts shaking every time I criticize them—they won't even put out leaflets listing all the symptoms; Richard, Dick, and Lennie owe their jobs somehow to the mayor; Dan is a schoolteacher; we're not allowed to say his last name out loud; the rest are just a bunch of disco dumbies. I warned you this was not a community that has its best interests at heart.

EMMA: But this is death.

NED: And the board doesn't want any sex recommendations at all. No passing along anything that isn't a hundred percent certain.

EMMA: You must tell them that's wrong! Nothing is a hundred percent certain in science, so you won't be saying anything.

NED: I think that's the general idea.

EMMA: Then why did you bother to start an organization at all?

NED: Now they've decided they only want to take care of patients—crisis counseling, support groups, home attendants . . . I know that's important, too. But I thought I was starting with a bunch of Ralph Naders and Green Berets, and the first instant they have to take a stand on a political issue and fight, almost in front of my eyes they turn into a bunch of nurses' aides.

EMMA: You've got to warn the living, protect the healthy, help them keep on living. I'll take care of the dying.

NED: They keep yelling at me that I can't expect an entire world to suddenly stop making love. And now I've got to tell them there's absolutely no such thing as safe sex . . .

EMMA: I don't consider going to the baths and promiscuous sex making love. I consider it the equivalent of eating junk food, and you can lay off it for a while. And, yes, I do expect it, and you get them to come sit in my office any day of the week and they'd expect it, too. Get a VCR, rent a porn film, and use your hands!

NED: Why are you yelling at me for what I'm not doing? What the fuck is your side doing? Where's the goddamned AMA in all of this? The government has not started one single test tube of research. Where's the board of directors of your very own hospital? You have so many patients you haven't got rooms for them, and you've got to make Felix well . . . So what am I yelling at you for?

EMMA: Who's Felix? Who is Felix?

NED: I introduced you to him at that Health Forum you spoke at.

EMMA: You've taken a lover?

NED: We live together. Emma, I've never been so much in love in my life. I've never been in love. Late Friday night he showed me this purple spot on the bottom of his foot. Maybe it isn't it. Maybe it's some sort of something else. It could be, couldn't it? Maybe I'm overreacting. There's so much death around. Can you see him tomorrow? I know you're booked up for weeks. But could you?

EMMA: Tell him to call me first thing tomorrow. Seven-thirty. I'll fit him in.

NED: Thank you.

EMMA: God damn you!

NED: I know I should have told you.

EMMA: What's done is done.

NED: What are we supposed to do—be with nobody ever? Well, it's not as easy as you might think. (*She wheels herself directly in front of him.*) Oh, Emma, I'm so sorry.

EMMA: Don't be. Polio is a virus, too. I caught it three months before the Salk vaccine was announced. Nobody gets polio anymore.

NED: Were you in an iron lung?

EMMA: For a while. But I graduated from college and from medical school first in my class. They were terrified of me. The holy terror in the wheelchair. Still are. I scare the shit out of people.

NED: I think I do, too.

EMMA: Learn how to use it. It can be very useful. Don't need everybody's love and approval. (*He embraces her impulsively; she comforts him.*) You've got to get out there on the line more than ever now.

NED: We finally have a meeting at City Hall tomorrow.

EMMA: Good. You take care of the city—I'll take care of Felix.

NED: I'm afraid to be with him; I'm afraid to be without him; I'm afraid the cure won't come in time; I'm afraid of my anger; I'm a terrible leader and a useless lover . . .

(*He holds on to her again. Then he kisses her, breaks away from her, grabs his coat, and leaves. Emma is alone.*)

Scene 9

A meeting room in City Hall. It's in a basement, windowless, dusty, a room that's hardly ever used. NED *and* BRUCE *wait impatiently; they have been fighting.* BRUCE *wears a suit, having come from his office, with his attaché case. Both wear overcoats.*

NED: How dare they do this to us?

BRUCE: It's one-thirty. Maybe he's not going to show up. Why don't we just leave?

NED: Keeping us down here in some basement room that hasn't been used in years. What contempt!

BRUCE: I'm sorry I let you talk me into coming here. It's not the city's responsibility to take care of us. That's why New York went broke.

NED: What we're asking for doesn't cost the city a dime: let us meet with the mayor; let him declare an emergency; have him put pressure on Washington for money for research; have him get the *Times* to write about us.

BRUCE: The mayor's not going to help. Besides, if we get too political, we'll lose our tax-exempt status. That's what the lawyer in your brother's office said.

NED: You don't think the American Cancer Society, the Salvation Army, any charity you can think of, isn't somehow political, isn't putting pressure on somebody somewhere? The Catholic Church? We should be riding herd on the CDC in Atlanta—they deny it's happening in straight people, when it is. We could organize boycotts . . .

BRUCE: Boycotts? What in the world is there to boycott?

NED: Have you been following this Tylenol scare? In three months there have been seven deaths, and the *Times* has written fifty-four articles. The month of October alone they ran one article every single day. Four of them were on the front page. For us—in seventeen months they've written seven puny inside articles. And we have a thousand cases!

BRUCE: So?

NED: So the *Times* won't write about us, why should we read it?

BRUCE: I read it every morning. The next thing you'll say is we should stop shopping at Bloomingdale's.

NED: We should picket the White House!

BRUCE: Brilliant.

NED: Don't you have any vision of what we could become? A powerful national organization effecting change! Bruce, you must have been a fighter once. When you were a Green Beret, did you kill people?

BRUCE: A couple of times.

NED: Did you like being a soldier?

BRUCE: I loved it.

NED: Then why did you quit?

BRUCE: I didn't quit! I just don't like being earmarked gay.

NED: Bruce, what are you doing in this organization?

BRUCE: There are a lot of sick people out there that need our help.

NED: There are going to be a lot more sick people out there if we don't get our act together. Did you give up combat completely?

BRUCE: Don't you fucking talk to me about combat! I just fight different from you.

NED: I haven't seen your way yet.

BRUCE: Oh, you haven't? Where have you been?

NED: Bruce, Albert may be dying. Why doesn't that alone make you want to fight harder?

BRUCE: Get off my back!

NED: Get off your ass!

(TOMMY *enters*.)

TOMMY: Wonderful—we finally get a meeting with the mayor's assistant and you two are having another fight.

BRUCE: I didn't have the fight, he had the fight. It's always Ned who has the fight.

TOMMY: Where the hell are we? What kind of tomb is this they put us in? Don't they want us to be seen above ground? Where is he? I'm an hour late.

NED: An hour and a half. And where's Mickey?

TOMMY: Not with me, lambchop. I've been up at Bellevue. I put a sweet dying child together with his momma. They hadn't seen each other for fifteen years and he'd never told her he was gay, so he didn't want to see her now. He's been refusing to see her for weeks and he was furious with me when I waltzed in with her and . . . It was a real weeper, Momma holding her son, and he's dead now. There are going to be a lot of mommas flying into town not understanding why their sons have suddenly upped and died from "pneumonia." You two've been barking at each other for an hour and a half? My, my.

BRUCE: Tommy, he makes me so mad.

NED: CBS called. They want our president to go on Dan Rather. He won't do it. They don't want anybody else.

BRUCE: I can't go on national television!

NED: Then you shouldn't be our president! Tommy, look at that. Imagine what a fantastic impression he would make on the whole country, speaking out for something gay. You're the kind of role model we need, not those drag queens from San Francisco who shove their faces in front of every camera they see.

BRUCE: You want to pay me my salary and my pension and my health insurance, I'll go on TV.

TOMMY: Both of you, stop it. Can't you see we need both your points of view? Ned plays the bad cop and Bruce plays the good cop; every successful corporation works that way. You're both our leaders and we need you both desperately.

NED: Tommy, how is not going on national TV playing good cop?

(MICKEY *enters*.)

MICKEY: I couldn't get out of work. I was afraid you'd be finished by now.

BRUCE: (*To* MICKEY.) Did you see his latest *Native* article?

MICKEY: Another one?

NED: What's so awful about what I said? It's the truth.

BRUCE: But it's how you say it!

MICKEY: What'd you say?

NED: I said we're all cowards! I said rich gays will give thousands to straight charities before they'll give us a dime. I said it is appalling that some twenty million men and women don't have one single lobbyist in Washington. How do we expect to achieve anything, ever, at all, by immaculate conception? I said the gay leaders who created this sexual-liberation philosophy in the first place have been the death of us. Mickey, why didn't you guys fight for the right to get married instead of the right to legitimize promiscuity?

MICKEY: We did!

TOMMY: I get your drift.

MICKEY: Sure you didn't leave anybody out?

NED: I said it's all our fault, every one of us . . .

(HIRAM KEEBLER, *the mayor's assistant, enters, and* NED *carries on without a break.*)

. . . and you are an hour and forty-five minutes late, so why'd you bother to come at all?

BRUCE: Ned!

HIRAM: I presume I am at last having the pleasure of meeting Mr. Weeks' lilting telephone voice face to face. (*Shaking hands all around.*) I'm truly sorry I'm late.

MICKEY: (*Shaking hands.*) Michael Marcus.

HIRAM: I'm Hiram Keebler.

TOMMY: Are you related to the folks who make the crackers? Tommy Boatwright.

BRUCE: Bruce Niles.

HIRAM: The mayor wants you to know how much he cares and how impressed he is with your superb efforts to shoulder your own responsibility.

BRUCE: Thank you.

NED: Our responsibility? Everything we're doing is stuff you should be doing. And we need help.

TOMMY: What Mr. Weeks is trying to say, sir, is that, well, we are truly swamped. We're now fielding over five hundred calls a week on our emergency hot line, people everywhere are desperate for information, which, quite frankly, the city should be providing, but isn't. We're visiting over one hundred patients each week in hospitals and homes and . . .

BRUCE: Sir, one thing you could help us with is office space. We're presently in one small room, and at least one hundred people come in and out every day and . . . no one will rent to us because of what we do and who we are.

HIRAM: That's illegal discrimination.

TOMMY: We believe we know that to be true, sir.

MICKEY: (*Nervously speaking up.*) Mr. Keebler, sir, it is not illegal to discriminate against homosexuals.

NED: We have been trying to see the mayor for fourteen months. It has taken us one year just to get this meeting with you and you are an hour and forty-five minutes late. Have you told the mayor there's an epidemic going on?

HIRAM: I can't tell him that!

NED: Why not?

HIRAM: Because it isn't true.

BRUCE: Yes, sir, it is.

HIRAM: Who said so?

TOMMY: The government.

HIRAM: Which government? Our government?

NED: No! Russia's government!

HIRAM: Since when?

MICKEY: The Centers for Disease Control in Atlanta declared it.

TOMMY: Seventeen months ago.

NED: How could you not know that?

HIRAM: Well, you can't expect us to concern ourselves with every little outbreak those boys come up with. And could you please reduce the level of your hysteria?

NED: Certainly. San Francisco, LA, Miami, Boston, Chicago, Washington, Denver, Houston, Seattle, Dallas—all now report cases. It's cropping up in Paris, London, Germany, Canada. But New York City, our home, the city you are pledged to protect, has over half of everything: half the one thousand cases, half the dead. Two hundred and fifty-six dead. And I know forty of them. And I don't want to know any more. And you can't not know any of this! Now—when can we see the mayor? Fourteen months is a long time to be out to lunch!

HIRAM: Now wait a minute!

NED: No, you wait a minute. We can't. Time is not on our side. If you won't take word to the mayor, what do we do? How do we get it to him? Hire a hunky hustler and send him up to Gracie Mansion with our plea tattooed on his cock?

HIRAM: The mayor is not gay!

TOMMY: Oh, come on, Blanche!

BRUCE: Tommy!

HIRAM: Now you listen to me! Of course we're aware of those figures. And before you open your big mouth again, I would like to offer you a little piece of advice. Badmouthing the mayor is the best way I know to not get his attention.

NED: We're not getting it now, so what have we got to lose?

BRUCE: Ned!

NED: Bruce, you just heard him. Hiram here just said they're aware of the figures. And they're still not doing anything. I was worried before that they were just stupid and blind. Great! Now we get to worry about them being repressive and downright dangerous.

BRUCE: Ned! I'm sorry, sir, but we've been under a great deal of strain.

NED: (*To* BRUCE.) Don't you ever apologize for me again. (*To* HIRAM.) How dare you choose who will live and who will die!

HIRAM: Now, listen: don't you think I want to help you? (*Confidentially.*) I have a friend who's dying from this in VA Hospital right this very minute.

NED: Then why . . . ?

HIRAM: Because it's tricky, can't you see that? It's very tricky.

NED: Tricky, shit! There are a million gay people in New York. A million and one, counting you. That's a lot of votes. Our organization started with six men. We now have over six hundred active volunteers and a mailing list of ten thousand.

HIRAM: Six hundred? You think the mayor worries about six hundred? A fire goes out in a school furnace on the West Side between Seventy-second and Ninety-sixth streets, I get three thousand phone calls. In one day! You know what I'm talking about?

NED: Yes.

HIRAM: If so many of you are so upset about what's happening, why do I only hear from this loudmouth?

NED: That's a very good question.

HIRAM: Okay—there are half a million gay men in our area. Five hundred and nine cases doesn't seem so high, considering how many of us—I mean, of you!—there are.

NED: This is bullshit!

BRUCE: Ned! Let me take it. Sir—

HIRAM: Hiram, please. You are?

BRUCE: I'm Bruce Niles. I'm the president.

HIRAM: You're the president? What does that make Mr. Weeks here?

BRUCE: He's one of the founders.

NED: But we work together jointly.

HIRAM: Oh, you do?

NED: Yes, we do.

HIRAM: Carry on, Mr. Niles.

BRUCE: Look, we realize things are tricky, but—

HIRAM: (*Cutting him off.*) Yes, it is. And the mayor feels there is no need to declare any kind of emergency. That only gets people excited. And we simply can't give you office space. We're not in the free-giveaway business.

BRUCE: We don't want it for free. We will pay for it.

HIRAM: I repeat, I think—that is, the mayor thinks you guys are overreacting.

NED: You tell that cocksucker that he's a selfish, heartless son of a bitch!

HIRAM: You are now heading for real trouble! Do you think you can barge in here and call us names? (*To* MICKEY.) You are Michael I. Marcus. You hold an unsecured job with the City Department of Health. I'd watch my step if I were you. You got yourself quite a handful here. You might consider putting him in a cage in the zoo. That I think I can arrange with the mayor. I'd watch out for my friends here if I were you. The mayor won't have it! (*Exits.*)

MICKEY: I don't believe this just happened.

NED: Mickey, I'm on the *Today Show* tomorrow and I'm going to say the mayor is threatening your job if we don't shut up.

MICKEY: The *Today Show!* You're going to do what?!

BRUCE: You can't do that!

NED: Of course I can: he just did.

BRUCE: God damn it, Ned!

NED: We're being treated like shit. (*He yells after them as they pick up their things and leave.*) And we're allowing it. And until we force them to treat us otherwise, we get exactly what we deserve. Politicians understand only one thing—pressure! You heard him—him and his three thousand West Side phone calls. We're not yelling loud enough! Bruce, for a Green Beret, you're an awful sissy! (*He is all alone.*)

Scene 10

EMMA's office. FELIX *sits on the examining table, wearing a white hospital gown.* EMMA *sits facing him.*

FELIX: So it is . . . it.

EMMA: Yes.

FELIX: There's not a little bit of doubt in your mind? You don't want to call in Christiaan Barnard?

EMMA: I'm sorry. I still don't know how to tell people. They don't teach acting in medical school.

FELIX: Aren't you worried about contagion? I mean, I assume I am about to become a leper.

EMMA: Well, I'm still here.

FELIX: Do you think they'll find a cure before I . . . How strange that sounds when you say it out loud for the first time.

EMMA: We're trying. But we're poor. Uncle Sam is the only place these days that can afford the kind of research that's needed, and so far we've not even had the courtesy of a reply from our numerous requests to him. You guys are still not making enough noise.

FELIX: That's Ned's department in our family. I'm not feeling too political at the moment.

EMMA: I'd like to try a treatment of several chemotherapies used together. It's milder than others. You're an early case.

FELIX: I assume that's hopeful.

EMMA: It's always better early.

FELIX: It also takes longer until you die.

EMMA: Yes. You can look at it that way.

FELIX: Do you want a second opinion?

EMMA: Feel free. But I'll say this about my fellow hospitals, which I shouldn't: you won't get particularly good care anywhere, maybe not even here. At . . . I'll call it Hospital A, you'll come under a group of mad scientists, research fanatics, who will try almost anything and if you die you die. You'll rarely see the same doctor twice; you'll just be a statistic for their computer—which they won't share with anyone else, by the way; there's not much sharing going on, never is—you'll be a true guinea pig. At Hospital B, they decided they really didn't want to get involved with this, it's too messy, and they're right, so you'll be overlooked by the least informed of doctors. C is like the *New York Times* and our friends everywhere: square, righteous, superior, and embarrassed by this disease and this entire epidemic. D is Catholic. E is Jewish. F is . . . Why am I telling you this? I must be insane. But the situation is insane.

FELIX: I guess we better get started.

EMMA: We have. You'll come to me once a week. There are going to be a lot of tests, a lot of blood tests, a lot of waiting. My secretary will give you a long list of dos and don'ts. Now, Felix, you understand your body no longer has any effective mechanism for fighting off anything?

FELIX: I'm going to be all right, you know.

EMMA: Good. That's the right attitude.

FELIX: No, I'm going to be the one who kicks it. I've always been lucky.

EMMA: Good.

FELIX: I guess everyone says that. Well, I'm going to be the one. I wanted a job on the *Times,* I got it. I wanted Ned . . . Have I given it to Ned?

EMMA: I don't know.

FELIX: Can he catch it from me now?

EMMA: We just don't know.

FELIX: Did he give it to me?

EMMA: Only one out of a hundred adults infected with the polio virus gets it; virtually everybody infected with rabies dies. One person has a cold, hepatitis—sometimes the partner catches it, sometimes not. I don't think we'll ever know why.

FELIX: No more making love?

EMMA: Right.

FELIX: Some gay doctors are saying it's okay if you use rubbers.

EMMA: I know they are.

FELIX: Can we kiss?

EMMA: I don't know.

FELIX: (*After a long pause.*) I want my mother.

EMMA: Where is she?

FELIX: She's dead. We never got along anyway.

EMMA: I'm going to do my damnedest, Felix. (*She starts to leave.*)

FELIX: Hey, Doc . . . I'll bet you say that to all the boys.

Scene 11

A small, crowded office. Many phones are ringing. TOMMY *is on two at once;* MICKEY, *going crazy, is on another, trying to understand and hear in the din; and* GRADY, *a volunteer, also on a phone, is trying to pass papers and information to either.*

MICKEY: Hello. Just a moment. It's another theory call. Okay, go ahead. Uranus . . . ? (*Writing it down.*)

GRADY: Whose asshole you talking about, Mickey?

MICKEY: Grady!

TOMMY: (*To* GRADY.) I thought your friend, little Vinnie, was going to show up today.

MICKEY: He had to go to the gym.

MICKEY: (*Reading into the phone what he's written.*) "Mystical electromagnetic fields ruled by the planet Uranus?" Yes, well, we'll certainly keep that in mind. Thank you for calling and sharing that with us.

GRADY: Harry's in a pay phone at the post office.

MICKEY: Get a number, we'll call him back.

GRADY: (*Into phone.*) Give me the number, I'll call you back.

TOMMY: (*Into one phone.*) Philip, can you hold on? (Into second phone.) Graciella, you tell Señor Hiram I've been holding for *diez minutos* and he called me. *Sí, sí!* (*Into first phone.*) You know where St. Vincent's is? You get your ass there fast! I'll send you a crisis counselor later today. I know you're scared, honey, but just get there.

(GRADY *hands* MICKEY *Harry's number.* TOMMY *has hung up one phone.*)

MICKEY: Well, call him back!

(BRUCE *comes in, dressed as from the office, with his attaché case.*)

TOMMY: Mickey, do we have a crisis counselor we can send to St. V's around six o'clock?

MICKEY: (*Consulting a chart on a wall.*) No.

TOMMY: Shit. (*To* BRUCE.) Hi, Bossman.

BRUCE: (*Answering a ringing phone.*) Hello. How ya doin'! (*To the room.*) It's Kessler in San Francisco.

GRADY: (*Into his phone.*) Louder, Harry! It's a madhouse. None of the volunteers showed up.

MICKEY: (*Busying himself with paperwork.*) Mystical?!

GRADY: (*On his phone.*) Oh, dear.

BRUCE: (*On his.*) No kidding.

GRADY: Oh, dear!

TOMMY: (*Picking up a ringing phone.*) Ned's not here yet.

BRUCE: (*To the room.*) San Francisco's mayor is giving four million dollars to their organization. (*Into phone.*) Well, we still haven't met our mayor. We met with his assistant about four months ago.

TOMMY: (*To* BRUCE.) Hiram called three days ago and left a message he found some money for us. Try and get him back.

MICKEY: We need to train some more crisis counselors.

GRADY: What about me, Mick?

TOMMY: (*Standing up.*) Okay, get this! The *Times* is finally writing a big story. Twenty months after the epidemic has been declared, the *Times* is finally writing a big story. Word is that

Craig Claiborne took someone high up out to lunch and told them they really had to write something, anything.

MICKEY: Who's writing it?

TOMMY: Some lady in Baltimore.

MICKEY: Makes sense. (*His phone rings.*) Hello.

GRADY: (*Still on his phone.*) Oh, dear.

TOMMY: Grady, darling, what the fuck are you oh-dearing about?

GRADY: (*Dropping his bombshell to Bruce.*) Bruce—Harry says the post office won't accept our mailing.

BRUCE: What! (*Into phone.*) Got to go. (*Slams phone down and grabs* GRADY's.) Harry, what's the problem?

MICKEY: (*Into his phone.*) That's awful.

BRUCE: (*Into his phone.*) They can't do that to us!

TOMMY: (*Who hadn't heard* GRADY.) What is it now?

GRADY: Harry went to the post office with the fifty-seven cartons of our new Newsletters—

TOMMY: Sugar, I sent him there!

GRADY: Well, they're not going anywhere.

BRUCE: (*To* TOMMY.) The post office won't accept them because we just used our initials.

TOMMY: So what?

BRUCE: In order to get tax-exemption we have to use our full name.

TOMMY: There is a certain amount of irony in all this, though not right now.

GRADY: He's double-parked and his volunteers had to go home.

TOMMY: Grady, dear, would you go help him out?

GRADY: No.

TOMMY and MICKEY: Grady!

GRADY: No! Why do I always have to do the garbage stuff?

MICKEY: Grady!

GRADY: Give me the phone. (*Into phone.*) Hold on, Harry, I'm coming to help you. (*To* TOMMY.) Give me cab fare.

TOMMY: Ride the rail, boy.

BRUCE: (*Into the phone.*) Harry, someone's coming. (*Whispering to* TOMMY.) What's his name?

TOMMY *and* MICKEY: Grady.

(GRADY *exits.*)

BRUCE: (*Into phone.*) Harry, bring them back. I want to fight this further somewhere. I'm sorry, I know it's a schlepp.

TOMMY: So this means we either pay full rate or embarrass their mailmen. Sorry, honey, I couldn't resist. (*Into phone.*) Graciella! (*To the room.*) How do you say "I've been holding twenty minutes" in Spanish? (*Into phone.*) City Hall is an equal-opportunity employer, doesn't that mean you all have to learn English? (*He hangs up.*)

MICKEY: (*Hanging up.*) That was Atlanta. They're reporting thirty cases a week now nationally.

BRUCE: Thirty?

TOMMY: The CDC are filthy liars. What's wrong with those boys? We log forty cases a week in this office alone.

BRUCE: Forty?

TOMMY: Forty.

MICKEY: Thirty.

BRUCE: (*Trying to decide how to enter this on the wall chart.*) So that's thirty nationally, forty in this office alone.

TOMMY: You heard what I said. (*Dialing, then into phone.*) Hi. Pick up for us, will you, dears? We need a little rest. Thank you. (*Hangs up.*)

(*There is a long moment of silence, strange now without the ringing phones.* TOMMY *lights a cigarette and sits back.* MICKEY *tries to concentrate on some paperwork.* BRUCE *is at the wall entering figures on charts.*)

BRUCE: Mickey . . . aren't you supposed to be in Rio?

MICKEY: Where's Ned?

TOMMY: He should be here by now.

BRUCE: I don't want to see him.

MICKEY: I need to talk to him. I don't want to lose my job because Ned doesn't like sex very much. He's coming on like Jesus Christ, as if he never took a lover himself.

BRUCE: Rio. Why aren't you in Rio?

MICKEY: I was in Rio. I'm tired. I need a rest.

BRUCE: We're all exhausted.

TOMMY: You're the president; you can't have a rest.

MICKEY: I work all day for the city writing stuff on breast-feeding versus formula and how to stay calm if you have herpes and I work all night on our Newsletter and my health columns for the *Native* and I can't take it anymore. Now this . . .

TOMMY: Take it slowly.

BRUCE: Now what?

MICKEY: I was in Rio, Gregory and I are in Rio, we just got there, day before yesterday, I get a phone call, from Hiram's office.

BRUCE: In Rio?

MICKEY: I'm told to be at a meeting at his office right away, this morning.

BRUCE: What kind of meeting? Why didn't you call me and I could have checked it out?

MICKEY: Because, unfortunately, you are not my boss.

BRUCE: What kind of meeting?

MICKEY: I don't know. I get to City Hall, he keeps me waiting forever; finally the Commissioner comes, my boss, and he said I hope you had a nice vacation, and went inside, into Hiram's office; and I waited some more, and the Commissioner comes out and says, Hiram doesn't want to see you anymore. I said, please, sir, then why did he make me come all the way back from Rio? He said, your vacation isn't over? I said, no sir, I was just there one day. I wanted to scream I haven't slept in two days, you dumb fuck! but I didn't. What I said was, sir, does this mean I'm fired? And the Commissioner said, no, I don't think he means that, and he left.

(NED *enters, unnoticed.*)

MICKEY: Ned's article in the *Native* attacking Hiram came out last week. I love sex! I worship men! I don't think Ned does. I don't think Ned likes himself. I—

NED: What are you trying to say, Mickey?

MICKEY: You keep trying to make us say things that we don't want to say! And I don't think we can afford to make so many enemies before we have enough friends.

NED: We'll never have enough friends. We have to accept that. And why does what I say mean I don't like myself? Why is anything I'm saying compared to anything but common sense? When are we going to have this out once and for all? How many cases a week now?

MICKEY: Thirty . . . forty . . .

NED: Reinhard dead, Craig dead, Albert sick, Felix not getting any better . . . Richie Faro just died.

MICKEY: Richie!

NED: That guy Ray Schwartz just committed suicide. Terry's calling all his friends from under his oxygen tent to say good-bye. Soon we're going to be blamed for not doing anything to help ourselves. When are we going to admit we might be spreading this? We have simply fucked ourselves silly for years and years, and sometimes we've done it in the filthiest places.

TOMMY: Some of us have never been to places like that, Ned.

NED: Well, good for you, Tommy. Maybe you haven't, but others you've been with have, so what's the difference?

TOMMY: (*Holding up his cigarette.*) It's my right to kill myself.

NED: But it is not your right to kill me. This is not a civil-rights issue, this is a contagion issue.

BRUCE: We don't know that yet, and until they discover the virus, we're not certain where this is coming from.

NED: We know enough to cool it for a while! And save lives while we do. All it takes is one wrong fuck. That's not promiscuity— that's bad luck.

TOMMY: All right, so it's back to kissing and cuddling and waiting around for Mr. Right—who could be Mr. Wrong. Maybe if they'd let us get married to begin with none of this would have happened at all. I think I'll call Dr. Ruth.

MICKEY: Will you please stop!

TOMMY: Mick, are you all right?

MICKEY: I don't think so.

TOMMY: What's wrong? Tell Tommy.

MICKEY: Why can't they find the virus?

TOMMY: It takes time.

MICKEY: I can't take any more theories. I've written a column about every single one of them. Repeated infection by a virus, new appearance by a dormant virus, single virus, new virus, old virus, multivirus, partial virus, latent virus, mutant virus, retrovirus . . .

TOMMY: Take it easy, honey.

MICKEY: And we mustn't forget fucking, sucking, kissing, blood, voodoo, drugs, poppers, needles, Africa, Haiti, Cuba, blacks, amebas, pigs, mosquitoes, monkeys, Uranus! . . . What if it isn't any of them?

TOMMY: I don't know.

MICKEY: What if it's something out of the blue? The Great Plague of London was caused by polluted drinking water from a pump nobody noticed. Maybe it's a genetic predisposition, or the theory of the herd—only so many of us will get it and then the pool's used up. What if it's monogamy? Bruce, you and I could actually be worse off because of constant bombardment of the virus from a single source—our own lovers! Maybe guys who go to the baths regularly have built up the best immunity! I don't know what to tell anybody. And everybody asks *me*. I don't know—who's right? I don't know—who's wrong? I feel so inadequate! How can we tell people to stop when it might turn out to be caused by—I don't know!

BRUCE: That's exactly how I feel.

MICKEY: And Ned keeps calling the mayor a prick and Hiram a prick and the Commissioner a prick and the President and the *New York Times,* and that's the entire political structure of the entire United States! When are you going to stop your eternal name-calling at every person you see?

BRUCE: That's exactly how I feel.

MICKEY: But maybe he's right! And that scares me, too. Neddie, you scare me.

TOMMY: If I were you, I'd get back on that plane to Gregory and Rio immediately.

MICKEY: Who's going to pay my fare? And now my job, I don't make much, but it's enough to let me help out here. Where are all the gay Rockefellers? Do you think the President really wants this to happen? Do you think the CIA really has unleashed germ warfare to kill off all the queers Jerry Falwell doesn't want? Why should they help us—we're actually cooperating with them by dying.

NED: Mickey, try and hold on.

MICKEY: To what? I used to love my country. The *Native* received an anonymous letter describing top-secret Defense Department experiments at Fort Detrick, Maryland, that have produced a virus that can destroy the immune system. Its code name is Firm Hand. They started testing in 1978—on a group of gays. I never used to believe shit like this before. They are going to persecute us! Cancel our health insurance. Test our blood to see if we're pure. Lock us up. Stone us in the streets. (*To* NED.) And you think I am killing people?

NED: Mickey, that is not what I—

MICKEY: Yes, you do! I know you do! I've spent fifteen years of my life fighting for our right to be free and make love whenever, wherever . . . And you're telling me that all those years of what being gay stood for is wrong . . . and I'm a murderer. We have been so oppressed! Don't you remember how it was? Can't you see how important it is for us to love openly, without hiding and without guilt? We were a bunch of funny-looking fellows who grew up in sheer misery and one day we fell into the orgy rooms and we thought we'd found heaven. And we would teach the world how wonderful heaven can be. We would lead the way. We would be good for something new. Can't you see that? Can't you?

TOMMY: I see that. I do, Mickey. Come on—I'm taking you home now.

MICKEY: When I left Hiram's office I went to the top of the Empire State Building to jump off.

TOMMY: (*Going to get* MICKEY's *coat.*) Mickey, I'm taking you home right now! Let's go.

MICKEY: You can jump off from there if no one is looking. Ned, I'm not a murderer. All my life I've been hated. For one reason or another. For being short. For being Jewish. Jerry Falwell mails out millions of pictures of two men kissing as if that was the most awful sight you could see. Tell everybody we were wrong. And I'm sorry. Someday someone will come along and put the knife in you and say everything you fought for all this time is . . . shit! (*He has made a furious, running lunge for* NED, *but* TOMMY *catches him and cradles him in his arms.*)

BRUCE: Need any help?

TOMMY: Get my coat. (*To* MICKEY.) You're just a little tired, that's all, a little bit yelled out. We've got a lot of different styles that don't quite mesh. We've got ourselves a lot of bereavement overload. Tommy's taking you home.

MICKEY: No, don't take me home. I'm afraid I might do something. Take me to St. Vincent's. I'm just afraid.

TOMMY: I'll take you wherever you want to go. (*To* BRUCE *and* NED.) Okay, you two, no more apologizing and no more fucking excuses. You two better start accommodating and talking to each other now. Or we're in big trouble.

MICKEY: We're the fighters, aren't we?

TOMMY: You bet, sweetness. And you're a hero. Whether you know it or not. You're our first hero.

(TOMMY *and* MICKEY *leave. There is a long moment of silence.*)

NED: We're all going to go crazy, living this epidemic every minute, while the rest of the world goes on out there, all around us, as if nothing is happening, going on with their own lives and not knowing what it's like, what we're going through. We're living through war, but where they're living it's peacetime, and we're all in the same country.

BRUCE: Do you want to be president?

NED: I just want Felix to live. (*A phone on* TOMMY's *desk rings.*) Hello. Hiram, old buddy, how they hanging? I want to talk to you, too. (*He listens, then hangs up softly.*) Tommy's right. All yelled out. You ready?

BRUCE: Yes.

NED: The mayor has found a secret little fund for giving away money. But we're not allowed to tell anyone where we got it. If word gets out we've told, we won't get it.

BRUCE: How much?

NED: Nine thousand dollars.

BRUCE: Ned, Albert is dead.

NED: Oh, no.

BRUCE: What's today?

NED: Wednesday.

BRUCE: He's been dead a week.

NED: I didn't know he was so close.

BRUCE: No one did. He wouldn't tell anyone. Do you know why? Because of me. Because he knows I'm so scared I'm some sort of carrier. This makes three people I've been with who are dead. I went to Emma and I begged her: please test me somehow, please tell me if I'm giving this to people. And she said she couldn't, there isn't any way they can find out anything because they still don't know what they're looking for. Albert, I think I loved him best of all, and he went so fast. His mother wanted him back in Phoenix before he died, this was last week when it was obvious, so I get permission from Emma and bundle him all up and take him to the plane in an ambulance. The pilot wouldn't take off and I refused to leave the plane— you would have been proud of me—so finally they get another pilot. Then, after we take off, Albert loses his mind, not recognizing me, not knowing where he is or that he's going home, and then, right there, on the plane, he becomes ... incontinent. He starts doing it in his pants and all over the seat; shit, piss, everything. I pulled down my suitcase and yanked out whatever clothes were in there and I start mopping him up as best I can, and all these people are staring at us and moving away in droves and ... I ram all these clothes back in the suitcase and I sit there holding his hand, saying, "Albert, please, no more, hold it in, man, I beg you, just for us, for Bruce and Albert." And when we got to Phoenix, there's a police van waiting for us and all the police are in complete protective rubber clothing, they looked like fucking astronauts, and by the time we got to the hospital where his mother had fixed up his room real nice, Albert was dead.

(NED *starts toward him.*)

Wait. It gets worse. The hospital doctors refused to examine him to put a cause of death on the death certificate, and without a death certificate the undertakers wouldn't take him away, and neither would the police. Finally, some orderly comes in and stuffs Albert in a heavy-duty GLAD bag and motions us with his finger to follow and he puts him out in the back alley with the garbage. He says, "Hey, man. See what a big favor I've done for you, I got him out, I want fifty bucks." I paid him and then his mother and I carried the bag to her car and we finally found a black undertaker who cremated him for a thousand dollars, no questions asked.

(NED *crosses to* BRUCE *and embraces him;* BRUCE *puts his arms around* NED.)

BRUCE: Would you and Felix mind if I spent the night on your sofa? Just one night. I don't want to go home.

Scene 12

EMMA *sits alone in a spotlight, facing a doctor who stands at a distance, perhaps in the audience. She holds a number of files on her lap, or they are placed in a carrier attached to her wheelchair.*

EXAMINING DOCTOR: Dr. Brookner, the government's position is this. There are several million dollars in the pipeline, five to be exact, for which we have received some fifty-five million dollars' worth of requests—all the way from a doctor in North Dakota who desires to study the semen of pigs to the health reporter on Long Island who is convinced this is being transmitted by dogs and the reason so many gay men are contracting it is because they have so many dogs.

EMMA: Five million dollars doesn't seem quite right for some two thousand cases. The government spent twenty million investigating seven deaths from Tylenol. We are now almost into the third year of this epidemic.

EXAMINING DOCTOR: Unfortunately the President has threatened to veto. As you know, he's gone on record as being unalterably and irrevocably opposed to anything that might be construed as an endorsement of homosexuality. Naturally, this has slowed things down.

EMMA: Naturally. It looks like we've got a pretty successful stalemate going on here.

EXAMINING DOCTOR: Well, that's not what we're here to discuss today, is it?

EMMA: I don't think I'm going to enjoy hearing what I think I'm about to hear. But go ahead. At your own peril.

EXAMINING DOCTOR: We have decided to reject your application for funding.

EMMA: Oh? I would like to hear your reasons.

EXAMINING DOCTOR: We felt the direction of your thinking was imprecise and unfocused.

EMMA: Could you be a little more precise?

EXAMINING DOCTOR: I beg your pardon?

EMMA: You don't know what's going on any more than I do. My guess is as good as anybody's. Why are you blocking my efforts?

EXAMINING DOCTOR: Dr. Brookner, since you first became involved with this—and we pay tribute to you as a pioneer, one of the few courageous pioneers—there have been other investigators... Quite frankly, it's no longer just your disease, though you seem to think it is.

EMMA: Oh, I do, do I? And you're here to take it away from me, is that it? Well, I'll let you in on a little secret, doctor. You can have it. I didn't want it in the first place. You think it's my good fortune to have the privilege of watching young men die? Oh, what's the use! What am I arguing with you for? You don't know enough medicine to treat a mouse. You don't know enough science to study boiled water. How dare you come and judge me?

EXAMINING DOCTOR: We only serve on this panel at the behest of Dr. Joost.

EMMA: Another idiot. And, by the way, a closeted homosexual who is doing everything in his power to sweep this under the rug, and I vowed I'd never say that in public. How does it always happen that all the idiots are always on your team? You guys have all the money, call the shots, shut everybody out, and then operate behind closed doors. I am taking care of more victims of this epidemic than anyone in the world. We have more accumulated test results, more data, more frozen blood samples, more experience! How can you not fund my research or invite me to participate in yours? A promising virus has already been discovered—in France. Why are we being told not to cooperate with the French? Why are you refusing to cooperate with the French? Just so you can steal a Nobel Prize? Your National Institutes of Health received my first request for research money two years ago. It took you one year just to print up application forms. It's taken you two and a half years from my first reported case just to show up here to take a look. The paltry amount of money you are making us beg for—from the four billion dollars you are given each and every year— won't come to anyone until only God knows when. Any way you add all this up, it is an unconscionable delay and has never, never existed in any other health emergency during this entire century. While something is being passed around that causes death. We are enduring an epidemic of death. Women have been discovered to have it in Africa—where it is clearly transmitted heterosexually. It is only a question of time. We could all be dead before you do anything. You want my patients? Take them! TAKE THEM! (*She starts hurling her folders and papers at him, out into space.*) Just do something for them! You're fucking right I'm imprecise and unfocused. And you are all idiots!

Scene 13

A big empty room, which will be the organization's new offices. BRUCE *is walking around by himself.* NED *comes in from upstairs.*

NED: This is perfect for our new offices. The room upstairs is just as big. And it's cheap.

BRUCE: How come, do you think?

NED: Didn't Tommy tell you? After he found it, he ran into the owner in a gay bar who confessed, after a few beers, his best friend is sick. Did you see us on TV picketing the mayor yesterday in all that rain?

BRUCE: Yes.

NED: How'd we look?

BRUCE: All wet.

NED: He's got four more hours to go. Our letter threatened if he didn't meet with us by the end of the day we'd escalate the civil disobedience. Mel found this huge straight black guy who trained with Martin Luther King. He's teaching us how to tie up the bridge and tunnel traffic. Don't worry—a bunch of us are doing this on our own.

BRUCE: Tommy got the call.

NED: Tommy? Why didn't you tell me? When did they call?

BRUCE: This morning.

NED: When's the meeting?

BRUCE: Tomorrow.

NED: You see. It works! What time?

BRUCE: Eight A.M.

NED: For the mayor I'll get up early.

BRUCE: We can only bring ten people. Hiram's orders.

NED: Who's going?

BRUCE: The Community Council sends two, the Network sends two, the Task Force sends two, we send two, and two patients.

NED: I'll pick you up at seven-thirty and we can share a cab.

BRUCE: You remember we elected Tommy executive director.

NED: I'm going.

BRUCE: We can only bring two.

NED: You just call Hiram and tell him we're bringing three.

BRUCE: The list of names has already been phoned in. It's too late.

NED: So I'll just go. What are they going to do? Kick me out? Already phoned in? Too late? Why is everything so final? Why is all this being done behind my back? How dare you make this decision without consulting me?

BRUCE: Ned ...

NED: I wrote that letter, I got sixty gay organizations to sign it, I organized the picketing when the mayor wouldn't respond, that meeting is mine! It's happening because of me! It took me twenty-one months to arrange it and, God damn it, I'm going to go!

BRUCE: You're not the whole organization.

NED: What does that mean? Why didn't Tommy tell me?

BRUCE: I told him not to.

NED: You what?

BRUCE: I wanted to poll the board.

NED: Behind my back—what kind of betrayal is going on behind my back? I'm on the board, you didn't poll me. I am going to that meeting representing this organization that I have spent every minute of my life fighting for and that was started in my living room, or I quit!

BRUCE: I told them I didn't think you'd accept their decision.

NED: (*As it sinks in.*) You would let me quit? You didn't have to poll the board. If you wanted to take me, you'd take me. I embarrass you.

BRUCE: Yes, you do. The mayor's finally meeting with us and we all feel we now have a chance to—

NED: A chance to kiss his ass?

BRUCE: We want to work from the inside now that we have the contact.

NED: It won't work. Did you get this meeting by kissing his ass? He's the one person most responsible for letting this epidemic get so out of control. If he'd responded with one ounce of compassion when we first tried to reach him, we'd have saved two years. You'll see . . . We have over half a million dollars. The *Times* is finally writing about us. Why are you willing to let me go when I've been so effective? When you need me most?

BRUCE: You . . . you're a bully. If the board doesn't agree with you, you always threaten to leave. You never listen to us. I can't work with you anymore.

NED: And you're strangling this organization with your fear and your conservatism. The organization I promised everyone would fight for them isn't fighting at all. It's become the gay est.

BRUCE: Maybe that's what it wanted to become. Maybe that's all it could become. You can't turn something into something it doesn't want to become. We just feel you can't tell people how to live.

NED: Drop that! Just drop it! The cases are still doubling every six months. Of course we have to tell people how to live. Or else there won't be any people left! Did you ever consider it could get so bad they'll quarantine us or put us in camps?

BRUCE: Oh, they will not.

NED: It's happened before. It's all happened before. History is worth shit. I swear to God I now understand . . . Is this how so many people just walked into gas chambers? But at least they identified themselves to each other and to the world.

BRUCE: You can't call people gay who don't want to be.

NED: Bruce—after you're dead, it doesn't make any difference.

BRUCE: (*Takes a letter out of his pocket.*) The board wanted me to read you this letter. "We are circulating this letter widely among people of judgment and good sense in our community. We take this action to try to combat your damage, wrought, so far as we can see, by your having no scruples whatever. You are on a colossal ego trip we must curtail. To manipulate fear, as you have done repeatedly in your 'merchandising' of this epidemic, is to us the gesture of barbarism. To exploit the deaths of gay men, as you have done in publications all over America, is to us an act of inexcusable vandalism. And to attempt to justify your bursts of outrageous temper as 'part of what it means to be Jewish' is past our comprehending. And, after years of liberation, you have helped make sex dirty again for us—terrible and forbidden. We are more angry at you than ever in our lives toward anyone. We think you want to lead us all. Well, we do not want you to. In accordance with our by-laws as drawn up by Weeks, Frankel, Levinstein, Mr. Ned Weeks is hereby removed as a director. We beg that you leave us quietly and not destroy us and what good work we manage despite your disapproval. In closing, please know we always welcome your input, advice, and help."

(BRUCE *tries to hand* NED *the letter.* NED *won't take it.* BRUCE *tries to put it in* NED'*s breast pocket.* NED *deflects* BRUCE'*s hand.*)

NED: I belong to a culture that includes Proust, Henry James, Tchaikovsky, Cole Porter, Plato, Socrates, Aristotle, Alexander the Great, Michelangelo, Leonardo da Vinci, Christopher Marlowe, Walt Whitman, Herman Melville, Tennessee Williams, Byron, E. M. Forster, Lorca, Auden, Francis Bacon, James Baldwin, Harry Stack Sullivan, John Maynard Keynes, Dag Hammarskjöld ... These are not invisible men. Poor Bruce. Poor frightened Bruce. Once upon a time you wanted to be a soldier. Bruce, did you know that it was an openly gay Englishman who was as responsible as any man for winning the Second World War? His name was Alan Turing and he cracked the Germans' Enigma code so the Allies knew in advance what the Nazis were going to do—and when the war was over he committed suicide he was so hounded for being gay. Why don't they teach any of this in the schools? If they did, maybe he wouldn't have killed himself and maybe you wouldn't be so terrified of who you are. The only way we'll have real pride is when we demand recognition of a culture that isn't just sexual. It's all there—all through history we've been there; but we have to claim it, and identify who was in it, and articulate what's in our minds and hearts and all our creative contributions to this earth. And until we do that, and until we organize ourselves block by neighborhood by city by state into a united visible community that fights back, we're doomed. That's how I want to be defined: as one of the men who fought the war. Being defined by our cocks is literally killing us. Must we all be reduced to becoming our own murderers? Why couldn't you and I, Bruce Niles and Ned Weeks, have been leaders in creating a new definition of what it means to be gay? I blame myself as much as you. Bruce, I know I'm an asshole. But, please, I beg you, don't shut me out.

(BRUCE *starts to leave, then stops and comes to* NED. *He puts his hand on his cheek, perhaps kisses him, and then leaves him standing alone.*)

Scene 14

NED'*s apartment.* FELIX *is sitting on the floor. He has been eating junk food.* NED *comes in carrying a bag of groceries.*

NED: Why are you sitting on the floor?

FELIX: I fell down trying to get from there to here.

NED: Let's put you to bed.

FELIX: Don't touch me! I'm so ugly. I cannot stand it when you look at my body.

NED: Did you go to chemo today?

FELIX: Yes. I threw it all up. You don't have to let me stay here with you. This is horrible for you.

NED: (*Touching* FELIX's *hair.*) No fallout yet. Phil looks cute shaved. I'm hungry. How about you? Can you eat a little? Please. You've got to eat. Soup ... something light ... I've bought dinner.

FELIX: Emma says a cure won't come until the next century. Emma says it's years till a vaccine, which won't do me any good anyway. Emma says the incubation period might be up to three, ten, twenty years.

NED: Emma says you've got to eat.

FELIX: I looked at all my datebooks and no one else I slept with is sick. That I know of. Maybe it was you. Maybe you've been a carrier for twenty years. Or maybe now you only have three years to go.

NED: Felix, we don't need to do this again to each other.

FELIX: Whoever thought you'd die from having sex?

NED: Did Emma also tell you that research at the NIH has finally started. That something is now possible. We have to hope.

FELIX: Oh, do we?

NED: Yes, we do.

FELIX: And how am I supposed to do that? You Jewish boys who think you can always make everything right—that the world can always be a better place. Did I tell you the *Times* is running an editorial this Sunday entitled "The Slow Response"? And you're right: I didn't have anything to do with it.

NED: Why are you doing this? Why are you eating this shit? Twinkies, potato chips ... You know how important it is to watch your nutrition. You're supposed to eat right.

FELIX: I have a life expectancy of ten more minutes I'm going to eat what I want to eat. Ned, it's going to get messier any day now and I don't want to make you see it.

NED: Nobody makes me do anything; you should know that better than anybody else by now. What are you going to do? Sit on the floor for the rest of your life? We have a bed in the other room. You could listen to those relaxation tapes we bought you three months ago. You haven't used them at all. Do you hear me?

FELIX: Yes, I hear you. That guy David who sold you the pig on Bleecker Street finally died. He took forever. They say he looked like someone out of Auschwitz. Do you hear me?

NED: No. Are you ready to get up yet? And eat something?

FELIX: No!—I've had over forty treatments. No!—I've had three, no four different types of chemo. No!—I've had interferon, a couple kinds. I've had two different experimentals. Emma has spent more time on me than anyone else. None of it has done a thing. I've had to go into the hospital four times—and please God don't make me go back into the hospital until I die. My illness has cost my—no! the *New Yorks Times'* insurance company over $300,000. Eighty-five percent of us are dead after two years, Alexander; it gets higher after three. Emma has lost so many patients they call her Dr. Death. You cannot force the goddamn sun to come out.

NED: Felix, I am so sick of statistics, and numbers, and body counts, and how-manys, and Emma; and every day, Felix, there are only more numbers, and fights—I am so sick of fighting, and bragging about fighting, and everybody's stupidity, and blindness, and intransigence, and guilt trips. You can't eat the food? Don't eat the food. Take your poison. I don't care. You can't get up off the floor—fine, stay there. I don't care. Fish—fish is good for you; we don't want any of that, do we? (*Item by item, he throws the food on the floor.*) No green salad. No broccoli; we don't want any of that, no, sir. No bread with seven grains. Who would ever want any milk? You might get some calcium in your bones. (*The carton of milk explodes when it hits the floor.*) You want to die, Felix? Die!

(NED *retreats to a far corner. After a moment,* FELIX *crawls through the milk, takes an item of food, which he pulls along with his hand, and with extreme effort makes his way across to* NED. *They fall into each other's arms.*)

NED: Felix, please don't leave me.

Scene 15

BEN'*s office.* FELIX, *with great effort, walks toward him. Though he looks terrible,* FELIX *has a bit of his old twinkle.*

FELIX: Thank you for seeing me. Your brother and I are lovers. I'm dying and I need to make a will. Oh, I know Neddie hasn't been talking to you; our excuse is we've sort of been preoccupied. It's a little hard on us, isn't it, his kind of love, because we disappoint him so. But it is love. I hope you know that. I haven't very much time left. I want to leave everything to Ned. I've written it all down.

BEN: (*Taking the piece of paper from* FELIX *and studying it.*) Do you have any family, Felix?

FELIX: My parents are dead. I had a wife.

BEN: You had a wife?

FELIX: Yes. Here's the divorce. (*He hands* BEN *another piece of paper.*) And I have a son. Here's . . . she has custody. (*He hands over yet another piece of paper.*)

BEN: Does she know you're ill?

FELIX: Yes. I called and we've said our good-byes. She doesn't want anything from me. She was actually rather pleasant. Although she wouldn't let me talk to my boy.

BEN: How is my brother?

FELIX: Well, he blames himself, of course, for everything from my dying to the state of the entire world. But he's not talking so much these days, believe it or not. You must be as stubborn as he is—not to have called.

BEN: I think of doing it every day. I'm sorry I didn't know you were ill. I'll call him right away.

FELIX: He's up at Yale for the week. He's in terrible shape. He was thrown out of the organization he loved so much. After almost three years he sits at home all day, flagellating himself awfully because he thinks he's failed some essential test—

plus my getting near the end and you two still not talking to each other.

BEN: Ned was thrown out of his own organization?

FELIX: Yes.

BEN: Felix, I wish we could have met sooner.

FELIX: I haven't much, except a beautiful piece of land on the Cape in Wellfleet on a hill overlooking the Atlantic Ocean. Ned doesn't know about it. It was to have been a surprise, we'd live there together in the house he always wanted. I also have an insurance policy with the *Times*. I'm a reporter for the *New York Times*.

BEN: You work for the *Times*?

FELIX: Yes. Fashion. La-de-da. It's meant to come to my next of kin. I've specified Ned. I'm afraid they might not give it to him.

BEN: If he is listed as the beneficiary, they must.

FELIX: But what if they don't?

BEN: I assure you I will fight to see that he gets it.

FELIX: I was hoping you'd say that. Can I sign my will now, please, in case I don't have time to see you again?

BEN: This will be quite legal. We can stop by one of my associates' offices and get it properly witnessed as you sign it.

FELIX: My little piece of paper is legal? Then why did you go to law school?

BEN: I sometimes wonder. You know, Felix, I think of leaving here, too, because I don't think anybody is listening to me either.

And I set all this up as well. (*A hospital bed is wheeled into stage center by two orderlies, wearing masks and gloves.*) I understand that the virus has finally been discovered in Washington.

FELIX: The story is they couldn't find it, so after fifteen months they stole it from the French and renamed it. With who knows how many million of us now exposed ... Oh, there is not a good word to be said for anybody's behavior in this whole mess. Then could you help me get a taxi, please? I have to get to the airport.

BEN: The airport?

FELIX: I'm going to Rumania to see their famous woman doctor. A desperation tactic, Tommy would call it. Does flying Bucharest Airlines inspire you with any confidence?

Scene 16

FELIX's *hospital room.* FELIX *lies in bed.* NED *enters.*

FELIX: I should be wearing something white.

NED: You are.

FELIX: It should be something Perry Ellis ran up for me personally.

NED: (*As* FELIX *presses a piece of rock into his hand.*) What's this?

FELIX: From my trip. I forgot to give it to you. This is a piece of rock from Dracula's castle.

NED: Reminded you of me, did it?

FELIX: To remind you of me. Please learn to fight again.

NED: I went to a meeting at the Bishop's. All the gay leaders were there, including Bruce and Tommy. I wasn't allowed in. I went in to the men's room of the rectory and the Bishop came in and as we stood there peeing side by side I screamed at him, "What kind of house of God are we in?"

FELIX: Don't lose that anger. Just have a little more patience and forgiveness. For yourself as well.

NED: What am I ever going to do without you?

FELIX: Finish writing something. Okay?

NED: Okay.

FELIX: Promise?

NED: I promise.

FELIX: Okay. It better be good. (BEN *enters the scene.*)

FELIX: Hello, Ben.

BEN: Hello, Felix.

(*Before* NED *can do more than register his surprise at seeing* BEN, EMMA *enters and comes to the side of the bed.*)

FELIX: Emma, could we start, please.

EMMA: We are gathered here in the sight of God to join together these two men. They love each other very much and want to be married in the presence of their family before Felix dies. I can see no objection. This is my hospital, my church. Do you, Felix Turner, take Ned Weeks—

FELIX: Alexander.

EMMA: ... to be your ...

FELIX: My lover. My lover. I do.

NED: I do.

(FELIX *is dead.* EMMA, *who has been holding Felix's hand and monitoring his pulse, places his hand on his body. She leaves. The two orderlies enter and push the hospital bed, through all the accumulated mess, off stage.*)

NED: He always wanted me to take him to your new house in the country. Just the four of us.

BEN: Ned, I'm sorry. For Felix ... and for other things.

NED: Why didn't I fight harder! Why didn't I picket the White House, all by myself if nobody would come. Or go on a hunger strike. I forgot to tell him something. Felix, when they invited me to Gay Week at Yale, they had a dance ... In my old college dining hall, just across the campus from that tiny freshman room where I wanted to kill myself because I thought I was the only gay man in the world—they had a dance. Felix, there were six hundred young men and women there. Smart, exceptional young men and women. Thank you, Felix.

(*After a moment,* BEN *crosses to* NED, *and somehow they manage to kiss and embrace and hold on to each other.*)

THE END

The Destiny of Me

A Play in Three Acts

For my brother,
Arthur Bennett Kramer.

*"I guess you could have lived without me.
I never could have lived without you."*

Thank you.
I love you.

I would like to thank Sanford Friedman, Bill Hart, and Morgan Jenness for their invaluable dramaturgical contributions; and Dr. Suzanne Phillips, Dr. Joseph Sonnabend, Dr. Howard Grossman, Dr. Anthony Fauci, Dr. Robert Gallo, and Richard Lynn for answering my hundreds of medical questions.

L.K.

The Destiny of Me opened on October 20, 1992, at the Lucille Lortel Theater in New York City. The Circle Repertory Company (Tanya Berezin, Artistic Director) production was presented by Lucille Lortel. It had the following cast:

Cast of Characters

(in order of appearance)

Ned Weeks Jonathan Hadary

Nurse Hanniman Oni Faida Lampley

Dr. Anthony Della Vida Bruce McCarty

Alexander Weeks John Cameron Mitchell

Richard Weeks David Spielberg

Rena Weeks Piper Laurie

Benjamin Weeks Peter Frechette

Director Marshall W. Mason

Sets John Lee Beatty

Costumes Melina Root

Lighting Dennis Parichy

Original Music Peter Kater

Sound Chuck London & Stewart Werner

Production Stage Manager Fred Reinglas

Originally produced in association with Rodger McFarlane and Tom Viola

Place: Just outside Washington, D.C.
Time: Autumn, 1992.

About the Production

As with all plays, I hope there are many ways to design *The Destiny of Me*.

The original New York production turned out to be much more elaborate than I'd conceived it in my head as I wrote it. As I worked with the director, Marshall Mason, I began to fear I'd written an undesignable play (not that there should ever be such a thing!).

On *The Normal Heart* I'd had the talent of the enormously gifted Eugene Lee, ever adept at solving problems of this nature in miraculously ingenious ways, and ways that were not expensive. I suspect that Eugene's design for *The Normal Heart*—the way he solved not dissimilar problems—has been utilized unknowingly all over the world, just from the participants in one production seeing photographs of another.

This time, and it was also a great gift, I had the opportunity to work with John Lee Beatty, who'd designed many of Marshall's other productions. John Lee is another kind of theatrical genius, as obsessed with minute details as Eugene is off-the-cuff. Our set was a realistic, technical marvel, with the scenes from the past zipping in and out on clever winches. We even had a sink on stage, with running water, so that the doctors and nurses and orderlies who were constantly coming into the hospital environment could wash their hands, as they would in a real hospital.

The elaborate apparatus for the medical treatment Ned is undergoing, as well as everything having to do with blood, was also worked out meticulously. I have not, in this published version, completely detailed all this medical minutiae, or the comings and goings of the nonspeaking hospital staff that the availability of a group of young Circle Rep interns allowed us to utilize in peopling our stage. Nor have I gone into too much detail about how the blood machinery looked and worked, beyond cursory descriptions.

I guess what I'm saying, and hoping, is that a lot of inventive ways will be found to deal with any problems designing and producing my play might raise—that there is no *right* way, and that, as in all theater, imagination is also one of the actors, and there are many ways to play the part.

A note about the songs Alexander sings to taunt his father in Act I: it is not essential that these be the particular songs, so long as the songs used are from this era, which is the end of World War II.

There are, for instance, a great many other Andrews Sisters' songs, available now on numerous CDs. I happen to be very fond of 'Victory Polka,' but it's hard to locate the Time-Life Music CDs that contain the only recording I know of it (the second CD or fourth cassette of the album: 'V-Disc, The Songs that Went to War, World War I Fiftieth Anniversary Collector's Edition').

The *South Pacific* songs are available on both the original Broadway cast recording or the soundtrack album of the film. The songs from *Show Boat* ('Where's the Mate For Me' and 'Make Believe') as well as the brief exchange of dialogue are best represented on the complete EMI *Show Boat* (CD 7491082) or (my favourite) on the soundtrack from the MGM film, *Till the Clouds Roll By* (Sony CD AK 47029).

Introduction

I began arranging for the production of *The Destiny of Me* when I thought I was shortly going to die. It's a play I've been working on for years—one of those "family" slash "memory" plays I suspect most playwrights feel compelled at some point to try their hand at in a feeble attempt, before it's too late, to find out what their lives have been all about. I figured it would be the last words of this opinionated author.

Not only did I think my play would be done while I was on my deathbed or after, I decided I would definitely leave word that it would not be done while my mother, who is now approaching ninety-three, was still alive. I certainly didn't want to be around to discover how she would react to the portrayal, by her fifty-seven-year-old homosexual son, of some fifty years of *her* life.

As destiny would have it, I appear to have received a respite from my expected imminent demise, at least one sufficient enough to ask myself: what have I gone and done?

I call *The Destiny of Me* a companion play to the one I wrote in 1985, *The Normal Heart*, about the early years of AIDS. It's about the same leading character, Ned Weeks, and the events of the earlier play have transpired before the curtain rises on the new one; it is not necessary, as they say, to have seen one to see the other. (The deathbed play remains to he written; now I have the chance to write a trilogy.)

Oh, I've had to make a few little changes. Instead of facing death so closely, Ned Weeks now only fears it mightily. And the hospital where he'd gone to die is now the hospital where he goes to try to live a little longer.

He still tries to figure out what his life's been all about.

This play now seems very naked to me. I'm overwhelmed with questions that didn't bother me before. Why was it necessary for me to write it? Why do I want people to see it? What earthly use is served by washing so much of "the Weeks family" linen in public?

When I wrote *The Normal Heart*, I had no such qualms. I knew exactly what I wanted to achieve and there was no amount of *anything* that could repress my hell-or-high-water determination to see that play produced, to hear my words screamed out in a theater, and to hope I'd change the world.

In what possible way could *The Destiny of Me* ever change the world?

About a dozen years ago I found myself talking to a little boy. I realized the little boy was me. And he was talking back. I was not only talking to myself but this myself was a completely different individual, with his own thoughts, defenses, and character, and a personality often most at odds with his grown-up self. These conversations frightened me. It's taken me years of psychoanalysis to rid myself of just such schizophrenic tendencies.

I found myself talking to this kid more and more. I found myself writing little scenes between the two of us. I was in trouble. I was falling in love with this kid. I, who face a mirror—and the world—each day with difficulty, had found something, inside myself, to love. I found myself writing this kid's journey—one that could only complete itself in death.

I should point out that I have always hated *anything* that borders on the nonrealistic. I hate science fiction and horror movies. I do not want to see a play, be it by Herb Gardner or Neil Simon or Luigi Pirandello, in which one actor (the author) talks to himself as embodied in another actor. My life has always been too bound up in harsh realities to believe in such fantastic possibilities, theatrical or otherwise. Nor have I ever been one to write comfortably in styles not realistic, not filled with facts and figures and *truth*. (Some readers tell me my novel, *Faggots,* is about as surreal a portrayal of the gay world as could be, but it was all the real McCoy to me.)

As I wrote on, in addition to worrying about my mother's reaction, I began to taunt myself with other fears. There is only one *Long Day's Journey into Night.* There is only one *Death of a Salesman.* And a million feeble attempts to duplicate their truth and to provoke their tears. And each playwright has only one family story to tell. And only one chance to tell it. Most, if they're lucky, throw their feeble attempts in the waste basket or file them with the stuff they plan to bequeath to their alma mater or unload on the University of Texas.

I further complicated my task by determining to write a personal history: a journey to acceptance of one's own homosexuality. My generation has had special, if not unique, problems along this way. We were the generation psychoanalysts tried to change. This journey, from discovery through guilt to momentary joy and toward AIDS, has been my longest, most important journey, as important as—no, more important than my life with my parents, than my life as a writer, than my life as an activist. Indeed, my homosexuality, as unsatisfying as much of it was for so long, has been the single most important defining characteristic of my life.

As I wrote of these journeys, and as we entered rehearsals, I found myself, over and over again, learning new things no amount of analysis had taught me. The father I'd hated became someone sad to me; and the mother I'd adored became a little less adorable, and no less sad. And although I'd set out, at the least, to have my day in court, actors, those magicians, grabbed hold of my words, and what had been my characters asserted themselves, and my harsh judgments were turned around in my face! My mother and father were showing me who they were, and not the other way around.

Oh, why had I written this damn play anyway!

I'd started out wanting to write a tragedy. I'd read all sorts of books that tried to define precisely what one is, including not a few that told me I couldn't write one anymore. I think the lives that many gay men have been forced to lead, with AIDS awaiting them after the decades-long journey from self-hate, is the stuff of tragedy. And I'd thought that the marriage my parents had was tragic, too; they could have had much better lives without each other.

But, once again, I discovered some surprising things. My younger self was very funny and spunky, and it's the me of today who, despite one hundred years of therapy, has lost resilience. As for my parents' lives, well, there is a difference between tragedy and sadness. I cannot bring myself to see my father as Willy Loman. Nor my mother as Medea or Clytemnestra or Antigone or Phèdre. Or Mary Tyrone. Or Joan of Arc. The stakes (pun intended) just weren't the same.

So was my determination to see this play produced a desire for vengeance? For blame? For catharsis? Was it only hubris? (Anita Brookner enunciated many writers' main motivation in the very title of one of her own books, *Look at Me.*)

I discovered long ago that writing doesn't bring catharsis. Writing *The Normal Heart* did not release my anger or make me hate Ed Koch and Ronald Reagan less or alter the present sorry state of the AIDS plague for the better. Writing *Faggots* did not find me true love or make me any more lovable or, so far as I can see, start any mass migration by the gay community to monogamous relationships. No, getting things off your chest doesn't get them off for very long.

Carole Rothman, the artistic director at Second Stage in New York, herself a parent, said she was uncomfortable about doing a play that "blamed" parents. (Joe Papp said he wouldn't put on any play where a father hit a son. I always thought this said more about Joe than my play.) "Blame" began to be a word that haunted me. Did I blame my parents? Is this what my play was saying? Over and over I reread my words. I wasn't blaming them. I was trying to understand what in their own lives made them the way they were and how this affected the lives of their children. I didn't see this as blame or vengeance.

In fact, I came to see their behavior as destined as my own. I even decided to change the play's title, which had been *The Furniture of Home* (taken from the same W. H. Auden poem as *The Normal Heart*). I don't know what sent me to Walt Whitman (beyond the desire to find my title in the words of another gay poet; I wonder now if it was as simple as one aging and physically deteriorating gay writer seeking inspiration from another), but I found myself reading and rereading his collected works. Sure enough, in "Out of the Cradle Endlessly Rocking," that haunting ode to life without love, I found what I was looking for—"the destiny of me."

Now I had a play and I had a title and I had a director— Marshall Mason. Then my leading actors, Colleen Dewhurst and Brad Davis, died. I lost my next leading man, Ron Rifkin, because of an unfortunate disagreement I had with the playwright Jon Robin Baitz. Ron, for whom Robbie wrote his greatest role, in *The Substance of Fire*, bowed out. It would be some time before Tanya Berezin of the Circle Repertory Company would read my play in March 1991 and immediately accept it. Like me by the men in my life, my play had first to have its own history of rejections: by the Public Theater (both Joe Papp and JoAnne Akalaitis), Manhattan Theatre Club, Lincoln Center, Playwrights Horizons (both André Bishop and Don Scardino), American Place Theater, Second Stage, Long Wharf in New Haven, Hartford Stage, Yale Rep (both Lloyd Richards and Stan Wojewodski, Jr.), South Coast Rep in California, the Goodman and Steppenwolf in Chicago, and Circle in the Square on Broadway.

I list these not to either tempt fate (oh, the nightmare possibility of those reviews that begin, "The numerous theaters that turned down Larry Kramer's new play were wise indeed . . .") or flaunt my rejections (*The Normal Heart, Faggots,* and my screenplay for *Women in Love* were originally turned down by even larger numbers), but to offer this thought to other writers, and to the little child inside that one talks to: almost more than talent you need tenacity, and an infinite capacity for rejection, if you are to succeed. I still don't know where you get these, even after writing this play to try to find the answer.

I guess that's what my play's about. I guess that's what my life's been about.

Not much of a message, huh? Well, maybe it's about a little more. I'll have to wait and see. Each day my family surprises me more and more. And that little boy inside me.

I'll bet you didn't expect Larry Kramer to talk like this.

I set out to make sense of my life. And I found out that one's life, particularly *after* one has written about it, doesn't make sense. *Life* doesn't make sense.

But change does. And there is no change without tenacity. And change is usually very hard. With precious few gratifications along the way to encourage you to carry on. And some change is good. And necessary. And some change must not be allowed.

This sounds more like Larry Kramer.

Yes, I can make sense out of *this*.

You may not agree, and you may not change your opinion, but you will have heard me make my case. And maybe, just maybe, you will think twice before slugging your kid tonight because he or she is gay, or you will not vote for any candidate who would allow AIDS to become a plague.

Yes, I know the possibilities are slim.

So what?

The little boy in me still believes everything is possible.

Mom, you taught me this.

And you lied.

But so does art and so does hope.

This article originally appeared in the *New York Times* Arts & Leisure section on Sunday, October 4, 1992.

O you singer solitary, singing by yourself, projecting me,
O solitary me listening, never more shall I cease
    perpetuating you,
Never more shall I escape, never more the reverberations,
Never more the cries of unsatisfied love be absent from me,
Never again leave me to be the peaceful child I was before
    what there in the night,
By the sea under the yellow and sagging moon,
The messenger there arous'd, the fire, the sweet hell within,
The unknown want, the destiny of me.

From "Out of the Cradle Endlessly Rocking"
Walt Whitman

Act One

(NED WEEKS, *middle-aged, enters a hospital room with his suitcase.*)

NED: I grew up not far from here. The trees were just being chopped down. To make room for Eden Heights. That's where we lived. That's what they named places then.

(HANNIMAN, *a nurse, pushes in a cart with medical stuff on it, including* NED'*s records. She is black.*)

HANNIMAN: The eleventh floor is our floor—Infectious Diseases. We ask that you don't leave this floor, or the hospital, or the Institute's grounds, or indeed go to any other floor, where other illnesses are housed. Dr. Della Vida says it's better to have you on our side. I tell him you're never going to be on our side. You're not here to cause some sort of political ruckus? Are you?

NED: (*Unpacking some books.*) What better time and place to read *The Magic Mountain?*

HANNIMAN: Are you?

NED: I'm here for you to save my life. Is that too political?

(DR. ANTHONY DELLA VIDA *enters. He is short, dynamic, handsome, and very smooth, a consummate bureaucrat. He beams hugely and warmly embraces* NED.)

TONY: Hello, you monster!

NED: I never understand why you talk to me . . .

TONY: I'm very fond of you.

NED: . . . after all I say about you.

HANNIMAN: "Dr. Della Vida runs the biggest waste of taxpayers' money after the Defense Department." In the *Washington Post*.

TONY: No, in the *Washington Post* he compared me to Hitler.

HANNIMAN: No, that was in the *Village Voice*. And it was "you fucking son-of-a-bitch of a Hitler."

TONY: Where was it he accused me of pulling off the biggest case of scientific fraud since laetrile?

NED: *Vanity Fair.*

TONY: (*Studying* NED'*s file.*) All your numbers are going down pretty consistently. You didn't listen to me when you should have.

NED: Ah, Tony, nobody wants to take that shit.

TONY: They're wrong.

NED: It doesn't work.

TONY: Nothing works for everybody.

NED: Nobody believes you.

TONY: Then why are you here?

NED: I'm more desperate. And you sold me a bill of goods.

TONY: You begged me you were ready to try anything.

NED: I asked you when you were going to strike gold with *something*. You've spent two billion dollars.

TONY: No, sir! You asked me if I had anything I would take if I were you.

NED: No, sir! You said to me, "I've got it." And I said, "The cure!" And you said, "If you quote me I'll deny it." You slippery bastard.

TONY: You're the slippery bastard!

HANNIMAN: Yep, he sure is on our side.

NED: (*Reading from a newspaper clipping.*) "Dr. Della Vida has discovered a method to suppress the growth of the virus in mice by 80–90% ..." The *New York Times*.

TONY: For over a decade you have mercilessly condemned that newspaper's coverage of this illness. Suddenly they're your experts?

NED: (*Another clipping.*) " ... reconstituted genes will he introduced in transfusions of the patient's own blood ... cells given new genetic instructions, to self-destruct if they are infected." *The Lancet.* (*A third clipping.*) "Conclusion: The success of this theory in *in vitro* experiments, followed by the successful inoculation of three West African sooty mangabey monkeys, leads one to hope that human experimentation can commence without further delay." The *New England Journal of Monkeys*. I'll be your monkey.

HANNIMAN: Don't say that. We have to guarantee each chimp a thirty-thousand-dollar retirement endowment. Their activists are better than your activists.

TONY: How have you been feeling? (*Starts examining* NED.)

NED: Okay physically. Emotionally shitty. We've lost.

TONY: You *are* depressed. That's too bad. You've been very useful.

HANNIMAN: Useful?

TONY: All your anger has kept us on our toes.

HANNIMAN: They have yelled at, screamed at, threatened, insulted, castigated, crucified every person on our staff. In every publication. On every network. From every street corner. Useful?

NED: Who is she? I've been infected for so long, and I still don't get sick. What's that all about? Everyone thinks I *am* sick. Everyone around me *is* sick. I keep waiting *to* get sick. I don't know why I'm *not* sick. All my friends are dead. I think I'm guilty I'm still alive.

TONY: Not everybody dies in any disease. You know that. Your numbers could even go back up on their own. Why is my hospital surrounded by your army of activists? Am I going to he burned at the stake if I can't restore your immune system?

NED: I'm not so active these days.

TONY: You?

NED: (*Softly.*) They don't know I'm here.

HANNIMAN: Why don't I believe that?

NED: What have we achieved? I'm here begging.

(NED *suddenly reaches out and touches* TONY's *face.* HANNIMAN's *back is turned.*)

This new treatment—you can't even stick it into me legally. Can you?

TONY: Ned—I do think I'm on to something. You've really got to keep your mouth shut. You've got to promise me. And then you've got to keep that promise.

NED: The world can't be saved with our mouths shut.

TONY: Give me lessons later.

NED: How long can you keep me alive? I've got work to finish. Two years. Can you do that?

TONY: You know there aren't any promises. Two years, the way you look now, doesn't seem impossible.

NED: How about three? It's a very long novel. Why are you willing to do this for me?

HANNIMAN: Because if it works, you'll scream bloody murder if anyone stands in his way. Because if it doesn't work, you'll scream bloody murder for him to find something else. That's *his* reasoning. Now *I* would just as soon you weren't here. Period.

TONY: (*To* HANNIMAN.) Give him the double d.d.b.m. (*Leaves.*)

NED: What's a double d.d.b.m.?

(*From the cart,* HANNIMAN *wields an enormous needle.* ALEXANDER, *a young boy, is seen dimly on the side. He's wet from a shower, and wrapped in towels. He comes closer to see what's going on.*)

HANNIMAN: Mice and chimps were easy. You're our first one who can talk back. Drop your drawers and bend over.

ALEXANDER: What's she doing?

NED: I want my mommy.

ALEXANDER: Mommy's not home yet.

HANNIMAN: You even wrote in *The Advocate* you'd heard I was a lesbian.

NED: You're Mrs. Dr. Della Vida?

(*She rams the hypodermic into his ass.*)

(*Screams.*) We consider that a compliment!

ALEXANDER: Why are you here? (*No answer.*) Please tell me what's happening!

HANNIMAN: (*Still injecting him.*) I think it takes great courage for you to set foot anywhere near here. My husband works twenty hours a day and usually sleeps the other four in one of these rooms. I'm pregnant and I don't know how. Or why. With the number of patients we're seeing, I'm bearing an orphan. (*Extracts the hypodermic and takes a larger one.*)

NED: That wasn't it?

(*She laughs. She administers the second needle even deeper. He screams again, louder.*)

ALEXANDER: Tell me what's going on!

NED: I'm starring in this wonderful play about euthanasia.

(HANNIMAN *finishes and leaves.*)

ALEXANDER: Where's Benjamin? Where's *anyone?* Don't you have any friends? At a time like this? Something awful's happening. Isn't it? (*No answer.*) Will you give me a hug?

NED: Get lost, Lemon.

ALEXANDER: Just remember—*I* was here. (*Leaves.*)

NED: (*Changing from his street clothes.*) What do you do when you're dying from a disease you need not be dying from? What do you do when the only system set up to save you is a pile of shit run by idiots and quacks? What do you do when your own people won't unite and fight together to save their own lives? What do you do when you've tried every tactic you can think of to fight back and none of them has worked and you are now not only completely destitute of new ideas but suddenly more frightened than you've been before that your days are finally and at last more numbered and finite and that an obit in the *New York Times* is shortly to be yours? Why, you talk yourself into believing the quack is a genius (*Massages his sore ass.*) and his latest vat of voodoo is a major scientific breakthrough. And you check yourself in. So, here I am. At the National Institutes of Quacks.

They still don't know how this virus works inside our bodies. They still don't know how this disease progresses and what really triggers this progression. They still don't know if the virus could be hiding someplace else—its major home might not even be in the blood at all. Finally, in total desperation, my kids out there prepared a whole long list of what they still don't know; we even identified the best scientists anywhere in the world to find the answers.

When we were on the outside, fighting to get in, it was easier to call everyone names. But they were smart. They invited us inside. And we saw they looked human. And that makes hate harder.

It's funny how everyone's afraid of me. And my mouth. And

my temper. They should only know I can't get angry now to save my soul. Eight years of screaming at one idiot to wake up and four more years of trying to get another idiot to even say the word can do that. They knew we couldn't keep up the fight and that eventually they'd be able to kill off all the faggots and spics and niggers. When I started yelling, there were forty-one cases of a mysterious disease. Now a doctor at Harvard is predicting a billion by the new century. And it's still mysterious. And the mystery isn't why they don't know anything, it's why they don't *want* to know anything.

So what does all this say about the usefulness of . . . anything?

Yes, the war is lost.

And I'd give anything to get angry again.

ALEXANDER: (*Reappearing, still wrapped in towel.*) You are not going to die!

NED: Go away.

ALEXANDER: If you die I die!

NED: Please go away.

ALEXANDER: I kept you alive for quite some time, thank you very much!

NED: Lemon—get the fuck out of here.

ALEXANDER: I was here first! Are you rich and successful and famous? Two of them? One? Did you fall in love? (*No answers.*) Every single second of my entire life I've wanted there to be somebody! I gave you great stuff to work with. How did you fuck it up? Excuse me for saying so, but I think you're a mess.

(*He goes to his Eden Heights bedroom. The walls are plastered with theatrical posters from hit shows*—South Pacific, Mister Roberts, A Streetcar Named Desire, The Glass Menagerie.)

(*To* NED *and the audience.*) Alexander the Great ruled the entire known world, from east to west and north to south! He conquered it, with his faithful companions. He was very handsome. He was very fearless. Everybody knew who he was and everybody loved him and worshiped him and cherished him. He was king of everything! (*Singing.*) "Give me some men who are stouthearted men who will fight for the right they adore!" Good evening, Mr. Murrow. Thank you for coming into my home. This is where I wrote my Pulitzer Prize play and this, of course, is where I practiced my Academy Award–winning performance. An Alexander can be anything he wants to be! Dressed up for battle in shining armor and a helmet and plumes, or a gorgeous purple royal cloak. (*Singing.*) "Who cares if my boat goes upstream, Or if the gale bids me go with the river's flow? I drift along with my fancy, Sometimes I thank my lucky stars my heart is free—And other times I wonder where's the mate for me?" (*Speaking dialogue.*) "Hello ."

NED: "How do you do? Are you an actress?"

ALEXANDER: "Oh, no. But I'd give anything if I could be."

NED: "Why?"

ALEXANDER: "Because you can make believe so many wonderful things that never happen in real life." (*Singing.*) "The game of just supposing is the sweetest game I know, Our dreams are more romantic, Than the world we see."

NED: (*Singing.*) "And if the things we dream about, Don't happen to be so ..."

ALEXANDER: "That's just an unimportant tech-ni-cality." *Show Boat* was the first show I saw on Broadway. (*Singing.*) "Only make believe I love you ..."

NED: "Only make believe that you love me ..." Oh, get dressed. Before Pop catches you.

ALEXANDER: I can be Henry Fonda in *Mister Roberts* or Cornelia Otis Skinner in *Lady Windermere's Fan.* The second balcony of the National Theater is only ninety cents and I go every other week when they change the show. I can be Ezio Pinza or Mary Martin in *South Pacific.* "One dream in my heart. One love to be living for ... " And I am performing on the biggest stage and everyone is applauding me like crazy. (*Bowing.*) Thank you. Thank you very much. Oh, Ned! Nobody I know is interested in what I'm interested in. And I'm not interested in what they're interested in.

NED: And you're never going to be able to accept or understand that.

ALEXANDER: Do you get in trouble when you try to find out things?

NED: Only if you're nosey.

ALEXANDER: I'm nosey.

NED: The best people are nosey.

ALEXANDER: Thank you. I ran away once. To New York. I used all my baby-sitting money. I'd see a Broadway show every day for the rest of my life. Mom traced me to Aunt Fran's just as I was leaving to see Judith Anderson in *Medea.* Ma said under no circumstances was I allowed to see a play about a mother who murders both her children.

NED: I said, Why not?

ALEXANDER and NED: Pop wants to murder me all the time.

ALEXANDER: (*Making a turban from a towel and singing.*) "I'm gonna wash that man right outa my hair, And send him on his way."

(*Sounds of* RICHARD WEEKS *coming home.*)

My God, Pop's home! (*Furiously getting dressed,* NED *helping him.*) I always say Hope for the Best and Expect the Worst. Ned, Alexander means Helper and Defender of All Mankind. Why'd you change my name?

NED: Alexander the Great died very young.

(RICHARD WEEKS *enters. He is almost the same age* NED *is now, but he looks much older. He is impeccably dressed. He puts down his newspaper and takes off his jacket and tie and cufflinks and rolls up his shirtsleeves. He keeps on his vest with its gold chain that holds his Phi Beta Kappa and Yale Law Journal keys. He comes across some of* ALEXANDER'S *comic books.*)

RICHARD: Come here, you!

ALEXANDER: (*From his room.*) I'm not home from school yet!

RICHARD: I warned you if I caught you buying comic books one more time I'd take away your allowance. You'll never get into Yale.

ALEXANDER: I'm going to go to Harvard.

RICHARD: You are not going to go to Harvard.

ALEXANDER: (*To* NED.) What am I supposed to say? Poppa, this strange man who lives down the block *gives* me the comic books. If I let him stick his finger up my tushie and suck my penis. He says he's in medical school and I'm helping him learn. Isn't it all right to have comic books if I don't spend my own money on them?

NED: Mordecai Rushmore.

ALEXANDER: Why do I have to lie? (*Entering, dressed.*) Hi, Pop. What's a penis? (*Grabbing the offending comic books.*)

RICHARD: (*Leaving to wash up.*) Look it up in the dictionary.

ALEXANDER: It isn't in the dictionary.

RICHARD: Then ask your mother. (*Exits.*)

HANNIMAN: (*Enters with a large bottle of pills.*) Take two of these every two hours. You have a watch. I won't have to remind you.

NED: (*As* ALEXANDER *stuffs the comics behind a book on a shelf.*) What are you doing?

ALEXANDER: I always hide them here.

NED: (*Reading the book's spine.*) *Psychopathia Sexualis* by Dr. Richard von Krafft-Ebing.

HANNIMAN: There seem to be more and more unusually dressed people gathering outside. What are they going to do?

NED: Look, can we please try and be friends?

ALEXANDER: Hey! I think if you're going to be with me, you really should be with me.

NED: I'm sorry if I upset you.

HANNIMAN: You're not sorry. You're scared shitless. (*Leaves.*)

RENA'S VOICE: Somebody please help me!

(RENA WEEKS *manages to open the front door, carrying large bags of groceries. She is in her forties. She wears a Red Cross uniform—skirt, jacket, and hat.*)

ALEXANDER: (*Helping her.*) Hi, Mom. Dad says to ask you what's a penis.

RENA: I told you.

ALEXANDER: Tell me again.

RENA: When you grow up, you'll insert it into the woman's sexual organ, which is called the vagina. The penis goes into the vagina and deposits semen into my uterus, and, if it's the right time of the month, pregnancy occurs, resulting, nine months later, in a child.

ALEXANDER: That's all?

RENA: What else would you like?

(RICHARD *returns, drying his hands on a towel, which he then puts around his neck. The telephone starts to ring.*)

RICHARD: Why are you so late?

RENA: You want to eat, don't you? Can't anyone else ever answer the phone?

RICHARD: Who calls me? (*Takes out some new money, peels a bill off.*)

RENA: (*Answering the phone.*) Hello.

RICHARD: I'm raising your allowance from fifty cents to one dollar.

ALEXANDER: (*Surprised.*) Thanks, Pop.

RENA: Oh, Mrs. Noble! This is Rena Weeks, Home Service Director, Suburban Maryland Chapter American Red Cross.

RICHARD: (*Trying to give the rest of the money to* RENA.) Count it. I got a raise!

RENA: (*Taking the money and putting it down.*) Could you possibly send some of your wonderful Gray Ladies to help us out driving our paraplegic vets to the ball game this Saturday while our regular volunteers work the monthly Bloodmobile?

RICHARD: I hate it that you work.

RENA: Yes, it is hard finding volunteers now the war is almost over.

(ALEXANDER *accidentally drops some canned goods.*)

RICHARD: That table cost two hundred dollars!

ALEXANDER: One hundred and seventy-five.

RENA: Yes, some other time. (*Hangs up.*)

RICHARD: They fired fifty more. Abe Lesser and his wife moved out of their apartment in the middle of the night. Nobody heard them leave. How could anybody not hear them leave?

(ALEXANDER *sits down and reads part of* RICHARD's *newspaper, unconsciously jiggling his leg up and down with increasing speed.* RENA *puts out a cold meal; in a hurry, she'll rush through the serving, eating, and clearing.*)

RENA: It's been a terrible day for tragedy.

RICHARD: Abe Lesser is no more a Communist than Joe DiMaggio.

RENA: We had a dreadful fire in Hyattsville.

RICHARD: I went to Yale with Abie.

RENA: Six entire families were burned out of everything they owned.

RICHARD: I don't want to hear about it.

RENA: I found shelter for all of them. Six entire families, Richard.

RICHARD: That's enough! I asked you not to talk about it.

ALEXANDER: Louella Parsons is very angry at Rita Hayworth.

RENA: (*Telling* ALEXANDER.) And I had to call a lovely young bride and break the news that her husband—he was just drafted, they didn't even have time for a honeymoon—he was killed on his very first training flight.

ALEXANDER: Louella says playing bold hussies only gets Rita into trouble.

RENA: His plane just fell from the sky.

RICHARD: Didn't you hear me!

RENA: She hadn't even started receiving his paychecks and he's dead!

ALEXANDER: Louella says she should start playing nice girls like Loretta Young.

RENA: Somebody has to take care of them!

RICHARD: And I never get a hot meal!

RENA: Oh, you do too get hot meals!

RICHARD: I like my tuna salad with egg and you know it!

RENA: I didn't have time to boil eggs!

ALEXANDER: But Rita says the bold and the brazen are the only parts they offer her.

(RICHARD *suddenly and furiously swats* ALEXANDER'*s leg with his part of the newspaper.*)

What'd I do now!

RICHARD: You're boring a hole in the rug!

ALEXANDER: Four hundred dollars.

RENA: Alexander, eat.

RICHARD: Five hundred dollars!

ALEXANDER: Four hundred and forty-nine ninety-five.

RICHARD: Isn't Ben coming home again?

RENA: I don't know.

RICHARD: Four hundred and ninety-nine ninety-five! Tax, delivery, and installation. He's Alexander again?

ALEXANDER: At least seven full weeks ago I changed my name to Alexander. Alex, which I thought suited me, was only the whim of a foolish child, a mere moment in time. And Benjamin has always, *always*, preferred Benjamin. You're the only one who insists on shortening him to Ben. And no, Benjamin is not coming home. He had football practice this afternoon, tonight he puts the school paper to bed, and then he's sleeping over at one of his chums. And, *and,* he has told me confidentially that he hates eating at home. With us. Everyone fights too much. (*Salts his food vigorously.*)

RENA: He didn't say any such thing.

RICHARD: (*Slapping* ALEXANDER's *band.*) You cannot put so much salt on everything! Do you want your stomach to fall apart when you grow up?

ALEXANDER and NED: I'll let you know when I grow up.

NED: It did.

RICHARD: (*To* NED.) What did I tell you? (*To* ALEXANDER.) Ben your bosom buddy? He doesn't even know you're alive.

ALEXANDER: He does so! (*Salts his food vigorously.*)

RICHARD: Do you see what he's doing?

RENA: Richard, please don't say things like that to the boy.

RICHARD: Am I talking to the wall?

RENA: They love each other very much. Benjamin was dying for a brother. He ran all the way to the hospital.

ALEXANDER: And when he saw me he said, "God, he's ugly. What a lemon!" Why do you always have to tell that story? (*Salts vigorously again.*)

RICHARD: I wash my hands of him. He's your son.

RENA: He's your son, too. I forgot to put any salt in, I was in such a hurry.

RICHARD: You always take his side.

RENA: There aren't any sides. We're all on the same side. We're a family.

RICHARD: Where's my Gelusil? My ulcer's acting up.

NED: Take Alka-Seltzer. It's the only thing that works for me. (*Gives* RICHARD *one.*)

ALEXANDER: Here it comes, Alexander's ulcer.

NED: Did they have Alka-Seltzer then?

RICHARD: (*Preparing it in one of* NED's *hospital cups.*) I get these pains in my gut and the doctor says there's no cure and I said, of course not, how can you be cured of your own son.

NED: Of course they had Alka-Seltzer then. Adam, Noah, Abraham, Moses—all the Jews took Alka-Seltzer.

RICHARD: You haven't shut up since the day you were born.

NED: The Jews *invented* Alka-Seltzer.

ALEXANDER: And I won't shut up until the day I die!

NED: Jesus took Alka-Seltzer.

RENA: Both of you stop it! Where did this fight come from?

ALEXANDER: (*To* RICHARD.) Why don't fights with Benjamin cause your ulcer? Why is it always Alexander's ulcer?

RENA: You fought with Benjamin?

ALEXANDER: When he won his appointment it didn't look like the war would ever be over.

RICHARD: I won't let him throw away a West Point education!

ALEXANDER: But now there's no point to West Point.

RICHARD: A war isn't over just because you say it's over.

NED: World War II ended in '45 and McCarthy was the early fifties. I'm not remembering this properly.

ALEXANDER: Yes, you are, you are! You're remembering it just fine.

NED: (*Starting to take some of the pills* HANNIMAN *left.*) I don't remember what I'm remembering.

ALEXANDER: Isn't that the point? I'll tell you when you're wrong.

NED: I'm sure you will. (*Noticing the container.*) He knows I won't take this poison! (*Pumps the nurse's bell.*)

RENA: Richard, you're going to have to work the Bloodmobile on Saturday.

RICHARD: I'll be goddamned if I'll work the Bloodmobile on Saturday or any other day.

RENA: Then you can drive the paraplegics to the ball game. Take your pick. And watch your language.

RICHARD: The Bloodmobile on Saturday, Sunday you teach at Temple, and I never get a hot meal.

RENA: Now I'm not supposed to teach at Temple? How else could we pay for Alexander to learn about the history of our people?

ALEXANDER: Don't blame that one on me.

RENA: It's bad enough living in a place where we're the only Jews. It was bad enough his not being bar mitzvahed. My mother would die if she knew.

ALEXANDER: How will she know? You made me write her how sad we all were she couldn't come all the way from L.A. to see me become a man and thank you for your generous check.

NED: (*To* RENA.) Do you know I think that was my first conscious lie?

RENA: (*To* NED.) I was only trying not to break my mother's heart.

(*Goes into her bedroom.*)

ALEXANDER: Mordecai Rushmore was my first lie.

NED: He was kind of humpy.

ALEXANDER: I don't have to tell you there are a lot of comic books hidden behind Dr. Krafft-Ebing.

NED: So you like it?

ALEXANDER: It feels good. Except when it's over. When it feels bad.

RICHARD: (*Taking the money* RENA *has left by the phone.*) I got a raise.

ALEXANDER: How could I be bar mitzvahed when I don't believe in God?

RICHARD: Why do you say things like that?

ALEXANDER: What's wrong with saying what you believe?

RICHARD: You're just an obnoxious show-off!

ALEXANDER: And you're my father!

(RICHARD *raises his hand to hit him.* ALEXANDER *moves adeptly out of the way.*)

Do you believe in God?

RICHARD: Of course I believe in God!

ALEXANDER: I don't know why. He hasn't been very good to you.

NED: (*Impressed.*) Did we learn how to fight from them?

RICHARD: Then go live in Hyattsville with those goddamned six dozen burned-out families on their goddamned training flights.

ALEXANDER: I didn't learn one thing from them! Not one goddamned thing!

NED: Then where did we come from?

ALEXANDER: We made it on our own! With lots of help from me!

HANNIMAN: (*Rushing in.*) What's wrong?

NED: (*To* ALEXANDER.) So we sprang full-grown from the head of Zeus?

HANNIMAN: Are you having some sort of drug reaction?

ALEXANDER: Yes!

NED: Yes! (*To* HANNIMAN.) I started an organization of activists. Slowly we have lessened from ten to two the years required for a drug to meander through your maze from that first spark in a scientist's eye to your much-sought-after Good House-keeping Seal. So what do you give us as our first reward? You have studied this rat shit in one hundred and fifty cities, on four continents, in a quarter-million suffering, desperate, doc-ile bodies. You have tested it alone, in numerous combinations, in high dose and low dose, in early intervention and late. You have spent over $300 million attempting to disguise the truth we told you seven years ago, based on our own experience using bootleg supplies we smuggled out of the factories of its manufacturer in the dead of night, that rat shit is rat shit. But do you listen to us? Of course not. We are not scientists. Our results are not based on "good science," "controlled" studies that cost $300 million. How dare you still dispense this . . . this . . . this rat shit?!

HANNIMAN: When will you tell us how you really feel? (*Angry.*) Why do you and yours always and automatically believe the worst about everything we do? This "rat shit" has become the standard of care against which we must test anything new. That's the only way we can find out if *anything* is better. And you know as well as I do that so far there's *nothing else* to use as a control! To measure new "rat shit" against! (*Looking out the window.*) Oh, why are you here! We're all doing the best we can. Do you want vengeance or do you want a cure!

NED: I'm here to try the top-secret experimental miracle your husband has up his high-tech ass to redeem his wretched reputation (*Brandishing the bottle again.*) before all of the billion presently predicted cases die. It's called a last-ditch stand.

HANNIMAN: You've already been given the first part of the top-secret experimental miracle. What do you think it was I rammed up your low-tech ass? And you have to take this with it. (*Getting a glass of water and practically ramming some pills down his throat.*) Because the protocol we've submitted to the seventeen committees Congress mandates must repeat must vote approval every time Tony pisses requires that you cannot take one without the other. You want to be saved? Shut your fucking mouth and let us save you our way. Swallow! (*Leaves when she sees he does.*)

(RENA *returns wearing a different uniform.*)

RICHARD: Now he doesn't believe in God.

RENA: Come with me tonight for a change.

ALEXANDER: All God is is just a little black book in the sky where it's written down exactly when we're going to die.

RENA: That's very original. Alexander, the dishes.

RICHARD: You're going out again?

ALEXANDER: That's all God is. A little black book.

RENA: You know tonight is my night for being a hostess to the servicemen at the Stage Door Canteen. Come with me. We could dance.

ALEXANDER: Saying when we're going to die.

RICHARD: I don't want to dance.

ALEXANDER: It sure would save a lot of time if I could read it right now.

RENA: We used to go everywhere. Mrs. Roosevelt might he there. And those Andrews Sisters.

ALEXANDER: Ma, I know all their songs!

RICHARD: I'm tired. Sometimes I feel real old, Rene.

ALEXANDER: Take *me*!

RENA: Don't say that. You'll talk yourself into it.

RICHARD: And like I'm not going to make it.

NED: (*Directed toward* RICHARD.) You're the same age I am now.

ALEXANDER: Don't you dare feel sorry for him!

RENA: You're fine and our health is fine and you finally have a full-time job. We're all fine.

NED: You have ... thirty years before you die ...

RENA: I feel I'm really doing something useful. I love my job.

RICHARD: Which one? You have so many.

RENA: I like helping people. Why does that bother you so? What's wrong with my feeling good? (*Starts clearing the table.*)

RICHARD: I don't feel good. I've never felt at home here. I can't wait to go back home.

NED: You can't retire for twenty years.

RICHARD: Nineteen.

NED: Amost twenty.

RICHARD: Nineteen and a half.

ALEXANDER: Nineteen and three-quarters.

RENA: (*To* ALEXANDER.) Didn't you forget something?

ALEXANDER: (*Giving her a ritual kiss.*) A kiss for the cook.

RICHARD: A kiss for the cook? What did she cook?

RENA: Washington is such a transient city. Everyone's always talking about going back to someplace else. Funny how nobody ever thinks this place is home.

ALEXANDER: We don't live *in* Washington. We live on the wrong side of the District Line. We are *of* the Capital of the United States but we are not *in* it.

RICHARD: We never should have left Connecticut. We're going back.

ALEXANDER: We are outsiders.

RENA: I like it here. People do all sorts of interesting, important things. I got a new assignment. I'm going to help avert the many accidents suffered by returning servicemen just out of military hospitals and with prosthetic limbs.

ALEXANDER: What's prosthetic limbs?

NED: (*Starts singing softly, then a little dance.*) "Blue skies, smiling at me ... "

RENA: Artificial arms and legs and hands. Made of wood and metal. When these wounded men go into stores, the sales personnel recoil in fear and horror. I'm going to be trained at the Pentagon! And then I'll be sent to department stores like Garfinkel's and specialty stores, like Rich's Shoes. And I'll bring these arms and hands and legs with me so the staff can see and feel them and then they won't be so frightened of them and they can come right up to these men and say, "May I help you, sir?"

ALEXANDER: Mom, that's very depressing. I know all the Andrews Sisters' songs!

RICHARD: That's very depressing.

ALEXANDER: Please!

(RENA *goes back into her bedroom.* ALEXANDER *begins to sing a medley of Andrews Sisters songs.*)

"Oh give me land lots of land under starry skies above ..."
"Drinking rum and Coca-Cola ... " "Don't sit under the
apple tree with anyone else but me ... " "There's going to
be a hallelujah day, When the boys have all come home to
stay ..."

RICHARD: Stop that.

ALEXANDER: (*Dancing, kicking high.*) "And a million bands begin to
play ..."

RICHARD: I said stop it!

ALEXANDER: "We'll be dancing the Victory Polka!"

NED: "Never saw the sun shining so bright..."

ALEXANDER: You like the way Fred Astaire dances.

RICHARD: You don't dance like Fred Astaire.

NED: "Noticing the days hurrying by ..."

ALEXANDER: How do you know I won't develop? Even Fred started
somewhere. "When you're in love, my how time flies ..."

(RICHARD *pounces on him suddenly, trying to restrain the dance movements. But the kid refuses* to *stop and* RICHARD *finds himself becoming more violent than he intended.*)

Poppa!

(RICHARD *lets go, shaking his head at what has come over him; he sits
down and stares into space, before taking up his paper again.*)

Why can't I do what I want to?

NED: (*Helping him up from the floor.*) That is probably the least satisfactorily answered question in the history of man.

ALEXANDER: (*Defiantly.*) Oh, I am going to do with my life every single thing I want to do I don't care what and you better, too!

(RENA *comes out wearing an outfit for hostessing at the Stage Door Canteen. She carries a wooden leg and an arm with a metal hook. She takes* NED's *hand and makes him touch the limbs.*)

RENA: I want my son to become a leader in the fight against discrimination and prejudice. Don't stay up too late. (*Unloads the limbs on* NED *and kisses him good night. Starting out, passing* RICHARD.) Last chance. It will cheer you up. (*Leaves.*)

RICHARD: Yes, I have a good job. Yes, the government is a good employer that'll never fire me if I keep my mouth shut.

(NED *gives the limbs to* ALEXANDER.)

(*Laying out utensils, bowl, and cereal for his breakfast.*) I supervise the documentation of all the ocean-going vessels that come anywhere near or leave our shores. I verify their seaworthiness. I study their manifests and any supporting documents. Then I make a decision. Yes or No. There's not much evidence of crime on the high seas anymore, so usually there isn't any reason to say No. Each day is like the one before. Each week and month and year are the same. For this I went to Yale and Yale Law School. For this I get up every day at dawn while everyone's asleep. So I can go through life stamping papers Yes. I got a raise.

ALEXANDER: So did I. Thank you, Poppa. (*Tries to hug him, still holding the limbs.*) Poppa, would you like me to get up early and have breakfast with you?

RICHARD: (*Taking the limbs from him and moving away.*) That's okay. You finish your homework, boy?

ALEXANDER: Yes, Poppa.

RICHARD: That's good. You've got to get into Yale. Good night, boy.

ALEXANDER: Good night, Poppa. Poppa . . .

(ALEXANDER *wants to kiss him and be kissed. But* RICHARD *goes into his bedroom, taking the limbs.*)

Does the fighting stop someday?

NED: No.

ALEXANDER: Does any dream come true? (*No answer.*) Should I stop wishing?

NED: (*Pause.*) A few dreams do.

ALEXANDER: You had me worried.

NED: Not many.

ALEXANDER: Are you afraid if you tell me the truth I'll slit my wrists?

NED: I wish you could know now everything that happened so you could avoid the things that hurt.

ALEXANDER: Would I do anything differently?

NED: I don't know if we can.

ALEXANDER: Then don't tell me. I guess it wouldn't be much fun anyway if I knew everything in advance. It *will* become fun . . . ? Oh, Ned, I want a friend so bad . . . ly!

NED: I know.

ALEXANDER: (*Taking out Dr. Krafft-Ebing and reading from it.*) "X, a young student in North Germany, began his sexual life in his thirteenth year when he became acquainted with another boy. From that point, he frequently indulged in *immissio penis in os,* although his ambition was always *penem viri in anum.* My advice was to strenuously combat these impulses, perform marital duties, eschew masturbation, and undergo treatment." You sort of get the feeling that, whatever it is, Dr. Krafft-Ebing doesn't want you to do it. Ned, who am I? Who can tell me?

NED: There isn't anyone.

ALEXANDER: I'll talk to Benjamin! Why haven't I done it before?

NED: (*Trying to hold him back.*) Alexander . . .

ALEXANDER: Let go!

NED: Don't tell Ben!

ALEXANDER: Benjamin is the most important person in my life.

NED: Not yet. You're not good friends yet.

ALEXANDER: We are too! Don't you say that too!

(*The lights change to nighttime. There is moonlight.* BENJAMIN, *in a West Point uniform and carrying a small duffel bag, comes home.* BENJAMIN *rarely raises his voice; his anger is inside of him and his quiet and serious determination is pervasive.*)

NED: Ben, you were so handsome.

(HANNIMAN *enters and turns on the light, breaking the mood. She carries a tray on which are four plastic cups, each with a different-colored liquid.*)

HANNIMAN: Before we extract your blood and process it to insert the necessary genetic material, we must determine if you are capable of being transfected—that is, hospitable to receiving our retroviruses containing new genetic instructions without becoming infected or infectious. Each colored liquid contains a different radioactive antibody tracer which will be able to locate that part of your declining immune system that will he the best host for our new virus. L'chaim. (*Handing him each glass and seeing that he empties each one completely.*) I thought you should know, since of course you don't, that those picketers outside, who, of course, aren't in any way connected with your being here, are growing in number. They have sleeping bags and seem to be camping out. Is something going to happen in the morning that's awful? Last year a bunch sneaked in and chained themselves to Tony's lab tables. The police had to saw off the metal legs before they could take them to jail. OMB charged our budget $300,000 for new tables so we have $300,000 less to save your life. (*As* NED *finishes by taking his pills.*) What a good boy. Now we'll be able to see if a straight path can be cleared. (*Turns out the light and leaves.*)

(BENJAMIN *crosses in the dark and turns on a light in the bedroom.* ALEXANDER *wakes up and throws himself into his arms.*)

ALEXANDER: Benjamin! I must talk to you! When you're not here, I talk to you from my bed to yours. Do you talk to me? (*No an-*

swer.) I pretend Mom and Pop are both dead in a car crash and you and I live together happily ever after.

BENJAMIN: Hey, cheer me up, Lemon.

ALEXANDER: Guess what I got voted in class? (*No answer.*) Most talkative. (*No answer.*) Oh, Benjamin, I have so much to say. It's imperative I talk to you.

(RICHARD, *in pajamas and slippers, enters, pulling on a robe.* RENA, *in nightgown and slippers only, follows, bearing a plate of brownies.*)

BENJAMIN: I'd hoped you, not Uncle Leon, would be there for my pretrial deposition. Not as my lawyer. As my father.

RICHARD: I almost died!

BENJAMIN: My trial was scheduled long before your operation. Your operation wasn't an emergency. I was court-martialed.

RICHARD: I had to go when the doctor was free.

RENA: He's very famous.

BENJAMIN: Uncle Leon showed up three days late. They put me in detention until he came. The first thing he said to me was: "Your daddy has more money to pay for a lawyer than you think." You went to Uncle Leon, after not talking to him all these years, so you wouldn't have to pay for a lawyer?

RICHARD: I don't know anything about the kind of law that governs the trouble you're in!

BENJAMIN: What else is there to know when your own son says he's innocent?

ALEXANDER: Benjamin, I must talk to you.

NED: He really does have something important in his own life right now. Try and understand.

RICHARD: How did you plead?

BENJAMIN: Not guilty.

RICHARD: I didn't expect you to listen to me. (*Pause.*) I almost died. Did you know that?

BENJAMIN: That's why I'm here. They don't just let you out of beast barracks. How do you feel?

RICHARD: They cut out my insides. I had a hemorrhage. I almost bled to death.

RENA: Then the nurse left a window open and he got pneumonia. There was a sudden summer storm. By the time we finally got back here this room was flooded. Alexander and I got down on our hands and knees and sopped up water all night.

BENJAMIN: If either of you has any notions of my staying at West Point, please disabuse yourselves of them immediately. Ma, please put on a robe.

RENA: That's very thoughtful of you, darling. (*To* ALEXANDER.) Get me my robe.

(ALEXANDER *rushes in and out so he won't miss anything.*)

RICHARD: Why are you deliberately choosing to fight the system!

BENJAMIN: Where do you find choice? I'm accused of turning my head all of two inches during a dress parade because the man next to me tripped. For this a lieutenant colonel, a major, a captain, eight cadets have spent two months haggling over whether it was really four inches instead of two inches. But in reality I lose a year of my life not because I turned my head at all but because my drill inspector, Lieutenant Futrell, hates Jews.

RICHARD: That's right. They don't like Jew boys. Why do you want to make so much trouble?

BENJAMIN: Why do you take their side?

RICHARD: It's your word against theirs.

BENJAMIN: He lied.

RICHARD: Yes, he called you a liar.

BENJAMIN: He called me a kike. At four-thirty in the morning, I was pulled out of my bed, and hauled naked out into the snow by a bunch of upperclassmen, and forced to stand up against a brick wall, which was covered with ice . . .

ALEXANDER: Poor Benjamin.

RENA: Such a good education going to waste.

BENJAMIN: Please stop saying things like that.

RICHARD: Can't you see how impossible it is to be the only one on your side?

BENJAMIN: Can't you see I don't mind being the only one on my side?

ALEXANDER: Neither do I! (*As* RICHARD *is about to turn on him.*) Why can't you believe my brother!

BENJAMIN: Thanks, boy. I guess it was too much to expect I'd have the support of my parents.

RENA: Don't say that.

BENJAMIN: Why not? You're asking me to say I'm guilty, when I'm not, and to allow such black marks to enter my permanent record, and to carry on as if nothing has happened. The only thing that keeps me going is some inexplicable sense of my own worth and an intense desire not to develop the habit of quitting.

NED: Where did we come from, Ben?

ALEXANDER: He's magnificent!

RICHARD: Go to bed!

ALEXANDER: Never!

BENJAMIN: I am going to *force* them into declaring me guilty or innocent. They will be compelled to disprove the validity of my word.

ALEXANDER: It's the only way.

BENJAMIN: And unless you are willing to back up my judgment, we shall be coming to a parting of the ways.

ALEXANDER: (*To* NED.) How can he not help me?

RICHARD: I thought you came home to see me because I almost bled to death. (*Starts to leave, then turns.*) My own brother! We were going to be partners for life. He threw me out at the height of the Depression. Your mother says I quit because he made my life so miserable that I had no choice but to resign. Her and her peculiar version of the truth. My own brother fired me! I loved him and looked up to him like he was God and that's what he did. Your mom and I couldn't afford the rent so we had to default on our lease and move to someplace cheaper and Leon, for some reason I could never understand, buys up the remainder of that apartment's lease and twenty years later when Mom dies and leaves her few bucks to me, Leon, my brother, sues me for the $3000 back rent we didn't have in our pocket to pay plus interest for the twenty years. What kind of brother is that? We were going to be partners for life. Yes, I sent for him to help save you in your troubles. He has connections in high places that I'll never have. He's the best lawyer I know, the best lawyer I ever knew and ever will. Even if I don't talk to him. (*Leaves.*)

RENA: (*Kissing* BENJAMIN *good night.*) Everything will be fine. (*Kissing* ALEXANDER *good night.*) I love you both very much. (*Picking up plate and offering brownies.*) I made your favorites. I warned him Grandma Sybil should have left her money equally to both her sons. The funny thing is, after Leon was paid back, all it bought me was a new winter coat. You would have thought she'd left us the Hope Diamond. There's nothing in the world my sons can't do. (*Leaves.*)

(BENJAMIN *strips down to his undershorts.* ALEXANDER *tries not to look at him, but peeks anyway.*)

ALEXANDER: Do you have a favorite song? (*No answer.*) "One dream in my heart, One love to be living for . . ." You're not coming home, are you?

BENJAMIN: (*Looking out the window.*) There's not much safety around. As best we can, Alexander, we've got to tough it out. I left home a long time ago.

ALEXANDER: How do I get out? (*No answer.*) "One love to be dreaming of . . ." Honestly, sometimes I think I live here all alone.

NED: You do.

ALEXANDER: Oh, shut up. Benjamin, I need help.

NED: Boy, you have some mouth on you.

BENJAMIN: I'm going to go to Yale. It's the surest way I know to get rich.

ALEXANDER: It didn't help Pop.

BENJAMIN: Yes, it did. He found his job down here through some classmate. He'd still be unemployed.

ALEXANDER: What am I going to do?

BENJAMIN: You'll be at Yale soon enough.

ALEXANDER: I can't wait *that* long!

BENJAMIN: You'd be better off at some small liberal-artsy place where they don't mind you being different.

ALEXANDER: (*Pause.*) You can see I'm different?

BENJAMIN: A blind man can see you're different.

ALEXANDER: (*Pause.*) How am I different? (*No answer.*) Please tell me.

BENJAMIN: Lemon, I'm in trouble. Let's get some shuteye. (*Turns out light.*)

ALEXANDER: "Close to my heart he came, Only to fly away, Only to fly as day flies from moonlight . . . "

(HANNIMAN *enters and yanks open the blinds, letting in the light. She has equipment for drawing blood.*)

HANNIMAN: Not a morning person? Now we take some tests. I thought you would be out there directing your troops. There are twice as many. Thousands. Speeches. Firecrackers. Bullhorns. Rockets. Red glares. Colored smoke. It actually was very pretty. Lots of men dressed up like nurses. There don't seem to be any TV cameras.

NED: That's too bad.

HANNIMAN: Isn't it. Over fifty arrests so far. Mounted police and tear gas. One of the horses crushed somebody's foot. Why don't you like my husband? Is it some sort of sin to work for the government? Do you have any idea how much work all this involves? Tony's been up all night, culturing healthy cells to mix with your unhealthy ones. Then they'll be centrifuged together so they can be put into your blood. Then, from this, additional cells will be drawn off, which then are also genetically altered, so that the infecting part is rendered harmless before it's put back into you. That's for the anti-sense part. To sort of fake out the infected cells and lead them over the cliff to their doom. If it works . . . Well, it's worked with a little girl with another disease. If it works on you . . . I don't let myself think how proud I'll be. Why don't they know out there that you're in here? (*No answer.*) Would they think you'd crossed over to the enemy? (*No answer.*) They hate us that much?

NED: Too many of us have been allowed to die.

HANNIMAN: Allowed?

NED: There's not one person out there who doesn't believe that intentional genocide is going on.

HANNIMAN: So. Their saint is now a sinner.

NED: A sinner. My late lover's ex-wife, Darlene, whom Felix hadn't seen for over fifteen years, and who had remarried immediately after their divorce an exceptionally rich man, turned up at the memorial service. She brought her own preacher from Oklahoma. Uninvited, he got up and delivered a sermon. To a church filled with hundreds of gay men and lesbians, he yelled out: "Oh, God, take this sinner, Felix Turner, for he knew not what he did." There was utter silence. Then I stood up and walked over and stood right under his nose and screamed as loud as I think I've ever screamed: "Felix Turner was not a sinner! Felix Turner was a good man! The best I ever knew."

ALEXANDER: (*Rushing in.*) Who's Felix Turner!

NED: In due course.

(ALEXANDER *withdraws.*)

Darlene drew herself up and marched right over to me and shouted even louder: "I now know that I have been placed on this earth to make you and all like you miserable for your sins." And we've been in court ever since, fighting over his will, which left everything to me. I was in love for five minutes with someone who was dying. I guess that's all I get.

HANNIMAN: (*Finishes taking blood.*) "The desires of the heart are as crooked as corkscrews."

NED: "Not to be born is the best for man." W. H. Auden.

HANNIMAN: I know.

NED: He was a gay poet.

HANNIMAN: Well, I agree with him anyway.

NED: How do you know that poem?

HANNIMAN: If I were one of your activists, I would respond to that insulting question: Go fuck yourself. But I am only a beleaguered nurse, with a B.A., an M.S., and a Ph.D., who is breaking her butt on the front lines of an endless battle, so I reply: Go fuck yourself. "This long disease, my life."

NED: Alexander Pope.

HANNIMAN: Not a gay poet.

NED: (*Taking more pills.*) These are making me sick to my stomach.

HANNIMAN: Take an Alka-Seltzer. (*Leaves.*)

ALEXANDER: (*Rushing back in.*) Did I hear you correctly? You were only in love for five minutes? That's terrible! What did you mean, That's all you get? Mommy! What's wrong with me?

(ALEXANDER *runs into her bedroom.* RENA *wears only a half-slip and is having trouble hooking her bra up in the back. He automatically hooks her up.*)

RENA: I need new brassieres. It's time to visit Aunt Leona. What's wrong?

ALEXANDER: I'm *different!* Even Benjamin says so.

RENA: Her company won't give her one extra penny from all the millions they make from her designs. They're hers! You see how impossible it is for a woman to be independent? "Different" doesn't tell me enough.

NED: Ma, why don't you put on a dress?

RENA: If you're going to become a writer, you must learn to be more precise with words.

NED: Do not sit half-naked with your adolescent son. Is that precise enough?

ALEXANDER: (*To* NED.) Why does it bother you guys so much? She does it all the time. I don't even look. (*To* RENA.) I don't want to be a writer anymore. *The Glass Menagerie* didn't win the Pulitzer Prize. Ma, how could they not know it was such a great play? They gave it to a play about a man who talks to an invisible rabbit. I'm going to be an actor.

NED: What do you mean, you don't look?

ALEXANDER: I look at Ponzo Lombardo. In gym. He's growing these huge tufts of pub-ic hair. Around his penis. Around his huge penis. Which she doesn't know how to tell me about and he tells me to look up in the dictionary.

NED: Pubic hair.

ALEXANDER: Pubic hair.

RENA: I was going to be an actress.

ALEXANDER: Around his huge penis.

NED: That you pronounced correctly.

RENA: I had an audition for a radio program. On NBC. Coast to coast.

ALEXANDER: You never told me that. What happened?

RENA: I was summoned to the station. Oh, I was so excited.

ALEXANDER: Then what happened?

RENA: I walked round and around the block.

ALEXANDER: Then what happened?

RENA: I walked around again.

ALEXANDER: You never went inside?

RENA: Benjamin was just a baby. I couldn't leave him.

NED: You were going to tell her how you feel so different.

ALEXANDER: But she could have become a star of the airwaves!

NED: She didn't become a star of the airwaves.

ALEXANDER: Mommy—isn't it a good thing . . . being different?

RENA: We're all different in many ways and alike in many ways and special in some sort of way. What are you trying to tell me?

ALEXANDER: Is it okay for me to . . . marry a . . . for instance . . . colored girl?

NED: Oh, for goodness' sake.

RENA: You know how important it is for Jewish people to marry Jewish people. There are many famous Jews—Jascha Heifetz and Dinah Shore and Albert Einstein and that baseball player your father's so crazy about, Hank Whatshisname. But we can't name them out loud.

ALEXANDER: Why not?

RENA: If they know who we are, they come after us. That's what Hitler taught us, and Senator McCarthy is teaching us all over again.

ALEXANDER: What if I find a colored girl who's Jewish?

(*She puts her hand to his forehead to see if he has a fever.*)

(*Breaking away.*) All I know is I feel different! From as long ago as I remember! You always taught me to be tolerant of *everyone*. You did mean it, didn't you? I *can* trust you?

RENA: Give me an example of what makes you think you're different.

ALEXANDER: I don't ever want to get married.

RENA: Of course you do. Everyone gets married. That's what you do in life. You get married. You fall in love with someone wonderful and you get married.

ALEXANDER: Are you really happy with Daddy?

RENA: Than with whom?

ALEXANDER: Cary Grant.

RENA: I never met Mr. Grant.

ALEXANDER: He's gorgeous.

RENA: Alexander, gorgeous is . . . well, it's a word that's better for me than for you.

ALEXANDER: Why can't I say gorgeous?

RENA: It's too . . . effusive for a man, too generous.

ALEXANDER: What's wrong with being generous? You would have been happier with Cary Grant, too. We could all have lived happily ever after in Hollywood—you and me and Benjamin and Cary. Why'd you settle for Richard Weeks?

RENA: Don't you think I love your father?

ALEXANDER: *I* don't.

NED: I actually said it out loud.

ALEXANDER: No, *I* said it out loud.

NED: Once again, I remind you, this is not what you set out to talk about.

ALEXANDER: But doesn't it fit in nicely?

RENA: I had lots of beaux. One was very handsome. But your father took me in his arms on our very first date and looked deep into my eyes and said, You're the girl I'm going to marry.

ALEXANDER: (*Cuddling seductively close to her.*) Tell me about the handsome one.

RENA: (*Running her hand along his leg.*) You're growing up so.

NED: Please, Ma.

RENA: You never tell me how much you love me anymore. You used to tell me all the time, Mommy, I love you more than anyone and anything in the whole wide world.

ALEXANDER: (*Touched and guilty.*) Oh, Mommy, I'm grown up now and I'm not supposed to say things like that.

RENA: Oh, silly billy, who says?

ALEXANDER: Please tell me what to do!

RENA: About what!

ALEXANDER: I've got to get ready for my Halloween Pageant.

(*He breaks away and runs into the living room, where he opens an old trunk.*)

HANNIMAN: (*Entering with medical cart.*) Now we take some blood.

(*She will take blood and put some in each of four containers.*)

NED: The straight path has been cleared?

(HANNIMAN *nods.*)

I am transfectious and not infectious?

HANNIMAN: Transfected. Now I didn't say that. That's our goal. And by all Tony's measurements and calculations, you appear to be—so far—a good candidate.

RENA: (*Pulling on a housedress and joining* ALEXANDER.) That's all that's left from when we were in Russia and they came after all the Jews and we had to run if we wanted to stay alive. You'd think they'd give us a rest. Why does someone always want someone else dead?

ALEXANDER: I'll bet the handsome one wasn't Jewish.

RENA: No, he wasn't.

ALEXANDER: What was his name?

RENA: Drew.

ALEXANDER: Drew.

RENA: Drew Keenlymore.

ALEXANDER: Drew Keenlymore! Oh! What did he do?

RENA: He was my professor.

ALEXANDER: A poor gentile.

RENA: No, he wasn't. He was from one of the oldest families in Canada and his brother was Prime Minister.

ALEXANDER: Oh, Mom! Did he take you in his arms and kiss you all over and say he wanted to marry you?

RENA: They didn't do things like that in those days.

ALEXANDER: You just said Pop did.

(*He is putting on Russian clothing from the trunk—a peasant blouse, skirt, sash, babushka, from* RENA'*s youth.*)

RENA: Your Aunt Emma married a gentile. Momma wouldn't talk to her for twenty years. (*Helps him.*)

ALEXANDER: Did you love Drew?

RENA: I had long auburn hair. Everyone said I was very pretty. I had many chances.

(HANNIMAN *exits.*)

ALEXANDER: What happened to him?

RENA: I met your father.

NED: Who comes home and finds you in a dress.

RENA: No, I knew him already.

ALEXANDER: And you never saw Drew Keenlymore again. (*Stuffs Kleenex from* NED'*s bedside table into the blouse to make breasts. To* NED.) Mickey Rooney did this in *Babes on Broadway.*

NED: You hate Mickey Rooney.

ALEXANDER: I'm not so crazy about Pop either.

NED: That is a motivation that had not occurred to me.

ALEXANDER: That's what we're here for, kid. (*Tosses him back the Kleenex box.*)

RENA: No. I saw him again.

ALEXANDER: You did?

RENA: He wrote me he was coming to New York. This was before you were born and Richard was still with Leon and it wasn't working out, Leon bullied Richard mercilessly, the one thing I always pray is you and Benjamin will never fight and always love each other—will you promise me?

ALEXANDER: Don't worry about that—what happened!

RENA: He took me to Delmonico's. I didn't have a nice dress. But I dressed up as best I could. I felt like a child, going back to my teacher, with a marriage that was in trouble, I shouldn't be telling you all of this, I wish you could like him more . . . There was no money! In the bank, in the country. Everyone was poor, except your Uncle Leon, he and Aunt Judith living so high off the hog, you should have seen their apartment, in the El Dorado, with two full-time maids. (*Gets some makeup from her vanity and puts some lipstick and rouge on him.*)

ALEXANDER: Go back to Delmonico's.

RENA: After lunch, Drew asked me to come back to his hotel. The Savoy Plaza.

ALEXANDER: And?

RENA: I didn't go.

ALEXANDER: Not again! Alexander Keenlymore, farewell!

RENA: I had a baby to feed.

ALEXANDER: Benjamin could have had two full-time maids! Momma, don't you want to be different?

(RICHARD *suddenly appears, home from work, exhausted. He is furious at what he sees.*)

RICHARD: What are you doing to him?

RENA: Don't use that tone of voice to me.

RICHARD: Look at him! He's a sissy! Your son is a sissy!

RENA: He's your son, too!

RICHARD: If he were my son, he wouldn't be wearing a dress. If he were my son, he'd come with me to ball games instead of going to your la-de-da theater. Your son is a sissy! (*Hits him.*)

RENA: Richard!

(RICHARD *hits him again.* ALEXANDER *is strangely passive.* RICHARD *corners him and can't stop swatting him.*)

Stop it!

RICHARD: Sissy! Sissy! Sissy!

NED: Why aren't you fighting back?

ALEXANDER: When he hit me last week I vowed I'd never talk to him again. (*Singing to himself.*) "Waste no time, make a switch, drop him in the nearest ditch ... "

RENA: This time I won't come back when you turn up begging.

NED: Never run from a fight.

ALEXANDER: "Don't try to patch it up, Tear it up, Tear it up . . ."

RICHARD: That was a million years ago in another lifetime.

ALEXANDER: "You can't put back a petal when it falls from a flower . . ."

RENA: I can do it again!

ALEXANDER: "Or sweeten up a fella when he starts turning sour. Oh, no! . . ."

RENA: It's never too late to correct our mistakes.

ALEXANDER: "Oh, nooooo!"

NED: (*To* RICHARD.) Daddy, why did you hit me?

RICHARD: You have an awful life ahead of you if you're a sissy.

NED: How do you know?

RICHARD: Everybody knows. (*To* RENA.) You want to see something? You who always defends her darling son. You want to see what he does to himself?

ALEXANDER: "If you laugh at diff'rent comics, If you root for diff'rent teams . . ."

(RICHARD *rips the skirt and underpants off him.*)

RENA: Stop tearing my dress! It's all that's left!

ALEXANDER: "Waste no time, Weep no more . . ."

RICHARD: I come home from the ball game, I smell this awful smell, like something died. I caught him. Rena, I really let him have it.

(RICHARD *is trying to get ahold of* ALEXANDER's *penis. It becomes a tussle of him almost getting it, and* ALEXANDER *evading his grasp just in time.*)

RENA: You hit him?

RICHARD: Of course I hit him!

ALEXANDER: "Show him what the door is for . . ."

RICHARD: He had his privates all covered up with depilatory cream!

ALEXANDER: "Rub him outa the roll call and drum him outa your dreams!" LET GO!

RICHARD: (*To* RENA.) Don't you even care?

RENA: I do care!

ALEXANDER: I'm the only boy in my entire class except Ponzo Lombardo who has any puberty hair and everybody laughs at him!

RICHARD: (*Starts ripping down the theater posters from the walls.*) Thank God at least I've got one son who's a man.

ALEXANDER: Don't! They're the most precious thing I have!

RICHARD: So this is what it takes to get you to talk to me.

RENA: Don't do that to the boy!

RICHARD: This is what we do to sissies.

(ALEXANDER *crawls around trying to smooth out his beloved posters and piece them back together.*)

ALEXANDER: It's Halloween! I wrote a play. Mr. Mills divided my scout troop, half into boys and half into girls. I didn't have any choice!

RICHARD: You wrote a play?

RENA: Tonight's his opening night. He invited us.

ALEXANDER: (*Screaming with all his might.*) I hate you!

RENA: Don't say that!

ALEXANDER: You taught me to always tell the truth!

NED: Go for it! (*Feels dizzy. Swallows more pills.*)

ALEXANDER: (*To* NED, *furious.*) Get me out of this!

RENA: Apologize to your father immediately!

ALEXANDER: (*To* RENA *and* RICHARD.) I hate both of you!

RICHARD: (*Really hitting him.*) Do what your mother says!

ALEXANDER: (*Grabbing the Russian shawl, stepping into women's shoes, and standing up to both of them.*) Go to hell! (*Running off, as best he can, yelling.*) Trick or treat! Trick or treat!

(HANNIMAN *rushes into the room. Her white coat is heavily bloodied.*)

HANNIMAN: Are you happy now? Look what your people did to me!

End of Act One

Act Two

(NED *enters in a wheelchair, singing an Andrews Sisters' song.* HANNIMAN, *in a clean white coat, wheels in a cart with a small insulated chest.* DR. DELLA VIDA *follows.* NED *carries a huge poster that reads* TONY AND GEORGE, YOU ARE MURDERING US *over big blow-ups of* DELLA VIDA *and George Bush. He holds it in front of the window, which provokes cheers from outside.*)

TONY: Why do they hate me?

HANNIMAN: These are all over the hospital. Plastered on the corridor walls, in the johns, in the cafeteria, in the Director's office. On the X-ray machines!

NED: (*Putting up the poster on a wall.*) I had my CAT scan lying under a picture of you. It was very sexy.

TONY: You wish. Get into bed.

(NED *does so.* HANNIMAN *pulls back a curtain along the wall, revealing elaborate equipment—a high-tech orgy of gleaming cylinders, dials, tubes, bells, and lights, all connected to a computer.*)

NED: This is it? Wouldn't it be easier if I just checked into a monastery and took sleeping pills?

TONY: You drown my wife in fake blood. You chop the legs off my lab tables. You've got some crazy gay newspaper up in New

York that claims I'm not even studying the right virus. They call me Public Enemy Number One. Why aren't you guys proud of me? If I'm not in my lab, I'm testifying, lobbying, pressuring, I'm on TV ten times a week, I fly to conferences all over the world, I churn out papers for the journals, I supervise hundreds of scientists, I dole out research grants like I'm Santa Claus—what more do you want?

(HANNIMAN *carefully takes a sack of blood from the container and gives it to* TONY. *He inserts it into part of the machine. They repeat the procedure for two more sacks.*)

NED: A cure.

TONY: I'm not a magician.

NED: Now's not the time to tell me. There's no end in sight. That's why they hate you. You tell every reporter you have enough money. That's why they hate you. You tell Congress you have everything you need. That's why they hate you. You say more has been learned about this disease than any disease in the history of disease. That's why they hate you. You say the President cares. That's why they hate you.

(TONY *and* HANNIMAN *attach* NED *to the machine.*)

TONY: He does care! He tells me all the time how much he cares!

NED: You asked me, I told you. You're the one in charge and you're an apologist for your boss. That's why they...

TONY: If I weren't, do you think I'd get *anything*! You don't understand the realities of this town.

NED: The reality of this town is that nobody can say the word "penis" without blushing.

(RENA, ALEXANDER, and RICHARD *enter. It's evening, shadowy, at a seaside boardinghouse in Connecticut, on Long Island Sound.*)

HANNIMAN: The President named him a hero.

NED: No comment. On the grounds he might murder *me*. Wait!

TONY: (*Pulling a lever to release the blood into* NED.) This construct is the first transfect of anti-sense. Competing protein mechanisms will effect a cross-reactive anti-self.

RENA: (*Talking into a pay phone on the wall. Dropping in coins with each call.*) Jane, we've finally made it!

NED: That's what we want?

TONY: That's what we want.

RENA: Get your date book out. You're first!

TONY: If we're lucky, it will screw up your reproductive process.

NED: I'd assumed that already was screwed up.

TONY: Of your *viral* load.

RENA: It's been the longest year.

NED: Tell me again there isn't any down side.

TONY: I never told you there wasn't any down side.

NED: You did too!

TONY: It's too late now.

ALEXANDER: (*To* NED.) Come with me.

TONY: (*Taking* NED'*s hand.*) Relax.

NED: (*Grabbing* TONY.) Tony, I'm afraid.

TONY: We're going to be just fine.

RENA: Friday night at seven! Perfect! We can hardly wait! (*Hangs up, enters the engagement in her date book.*)

ALEXANDER: Ned, come back. Only two more weeks to Yale! No more Eden Heights. My new life! We don't have much time left before I grow into you and you kick me out. (*Pulls* NED *with him.*) Come on!

(TONY *and* HANNIMAN *leave.* ALEXANDER *helps* NED, *still connected by tubes to the machinery, get out of bed and walk to sit beside* RICHARD *on a porch swing.*)

NED: (*Applying salt liberally to some food.*) Hi, Poppa.

RENA: (*To* RICHARD, *as she dials another number.*) Jane and Barney are taking us to their new country club that costs a thousand dollars a year per family just to join. (*Into phone.*) Grace, darling, this is Rena! Just this minute! Tell me when you're free!

ALEXANDER: (*To the audience.*) Every summer we come back to Connecticut for two weeks at Mrs. Pennington's Seaside Boarding House, and every year everyone Mom and Pop grew up with has become richer and richer.

(RICHARD *grabs the salt away from* NED.)

(*To* NED.) Did I say that well?

NED: First-rate. And every summer you feel more and more different.

ALEXANDER: (*To the audience.*) And every summer I feel more and more frightened. Of what I don't know.

RENA: A swim in your new pool and lobsters for luncheon! Saturday at noon. We can hardly wait! (*She hangs up, enters the engagement, checks her address book, and dials another number.*)

(NED *grabs the salt back from* RICHARD.)

Grace and Percy bought that big estate in Westport.

(RICHARD *grabs the salt back from* NED.)

Cole Porter wrote some famous song there.

(NED *grabs the salt back from* RICHARD.)

NED: I want to eat it the way I want to eat it.

RENA: Percy sold his business for a million dollars and retired.

RICHARD: Who's going to pay the bills when you get sick?

NED and ALEXANDER: I'll let you know when I get sick.

ALEXANDER: Tradition means a great deal in our family.

RENA: Dolores, darling, this is Rena! Quiet, both of you! Oh, my God! (*To* RICHARD.) Dolores and Nathan are going around the world for an entire year.

RICHARD: I can't take it anymore. (*To* NED.) Why are you always so ungrateful?

RENA: I've always dreamed of a trip like that.

NED: Everything you always blame me for demands I defend myself.

ALEXANDER: You're playing me really well.

RICHARD: Blame? What are you talking about? (*Grabs the salt back.*) Blame!

RENA: An informal candlelight dinner for fifty on your outdoor terrace under the stars! Saturday at nine. You'll send a car and driver! We can hardly wait! (*Slamming down the phone.*) I've heard this fight for the last time! This is supposed to be a wonderful vacation! I've been on the phone calling people I haven't seen or spoken to or heard from in a year. Why don't you ever call them? They're your old childhood chums, too. I feel like such a suppliant. Inviting people to take us out and feed us. (*Having dialed another number.*) Tessie, it's Rena!

RICHARD: What I need's a vacation from him.

RENA: Are you free on Sunday?

ALEXANDER: Just two more weeks you won't ever have to see me again.

RENA: Don't say that!

RICHARD: Maybe then I'll feel better. Where's Ben?

RENA: You think he confides in me? (*Into phone.*) A cruise on your *yacht?* Cocktails at five to watch the sunset. We can hardly wait. (*Hangs up.*) Tessie and Isadore have a yacht.

(NED *suddenly feels a little woozy. He stands up uncertainly. A bell rings softly. A yellow light goes on. He indicates to a concerned* ALEXANDER *that he should carry on. He makes his way back to bed.*)

ALEXANDER: Benjamin is driving from New Haven in the new second-hand Ford he bought with his own money. He has jobs and he has scholarships and he's paying his own way and he's free, he's a free man, ever since he beat West Point and they said he wasn't a liar. So what do you know what's right for him or me or anybody? He won! My brother, whom you said wouldn't win, won!

(RICHARD *is standing directly in front of him.* ALEXANDER *holds his ground.* RICHARD *turns and leaves.*)

RENA: Who.

ALEXANDER: Who. (*Trying to kiss* RENA.) A kiss for the cook. (*As she pointedly ignores him.*) Now, Alexander, you know I don't like it when you talk back to your father like that. Yes, Momma, I know. I know you didn't mean it, dear. But I did mean it, Momma. Oh, boy, did I mean it. And I don't think I did anything wrong. Well, you can do your mom a great big favor. Even if you don't mean it. Just do it for me. For the Mommy you love. I will not apologize! Ever!

(*The yellow light goes off.*)

RENA: You used to say, Mommy, I'll do anything you ask me.

ALEXANDER: Ma, every kid says that.

RENA: Oh, do they? What else do they say?

NED: Mommy, I am going to become so famous someday, just so I can get away from here!

RENA: My last case before we left was a family without a father. They lived in a shack. The lovely young mother. With two adorable children. Who threw up all over the house. And bled all over the sheets. From some strange illness.

NED: And I must never forget that those two diseased babies might have been me and Benjamin.

RENA: The point is we're all healthy and together and he loves you very much.

NED: The point is in my entire life I never believed for one single minute that my father ever loved me. The point is I can't even figure out if I've ever been loved at all.

(ALEXANDER *is troubled by this.*)

RENA: The point is I love him and I love you and he loves me and he loves you and we all love each other very very much!

(ALEXANDER *goes to sit on the swing.*)

I was so proud, being asked to be an official hostess. But you didn't dance with your own mother at your own graduation prom, not once.

ALEXANDER: Nobody danced with their *mother*!

RENA: Bernie Krukoff did. Neil Nelson did. Skipper with the red hair did. Do you know how much I wanted you? Do you? Mr. Know-It-All. You think you know it all. Some things you don't know.

ALEXANDER: You told me about Drew Keenlymore.

RENA: I did not.

NED: You did, too.

ALEXANDER: Before I found his letters.

RENA: I don't even know where they are.

NED: Hidden in a navy crocheted purse inside an old Macy's hatbox at the back of the top of your bedroom closet, over on the far right.

ALEXANDER: The purse is cable stitch.

RENA: Your great-grandmother crocheted that purse. She was married three times and she divorced each one of them. She traveled all over the world. And then she came home and my poppa took care of her until the day she died. She was ninety-nine. She was one gutsy lady.

NED: She was one scary lady. Always reading her Bible out loud, day and night, and barking orders in Hebrew.

ALEXANDER: Grandma Sybil was the scary one!

RENA: (*Sitting between them.*) After we got married, your Grandmother Sybil made Daddy promise he'd never leave her, that one of her sons would always look out for her. Richard kept his promise, which is why she left him the money. He worshiped her. Her great sinful secret was her husband's infidelity. What was his name? I can't even remember his name. She would never let his name be said out loud. She threw him out for sleeping with another woman. Kicked him out. Just like that. Judith divorced Leon, too. He kissed his mistress in his and Judith's very bedroom. I caught them accidentally. He laughed at me! "Why don't you go out and have some pleasure in life? Why are you always so faithful to that loser?" Imagine saying that about your own brother? I'd been to a doctor. The doctor examined me and told me I wasn't pregnant. Richard—where was Richard? Well, he wasn't there and I'd gone to spend the night with Mother Sybil. She terrified me, too. She was a mean, unloving, self-centered . . . bitch. Grandma Sybil only had one bed. I had to sleep with her. Oh, her smells! Her old-lady unguents and liniments. Don't open the window. I feel a draft. I feel a draft. She started talking to me in the dark. Telling me how much she'd loved him. Her husband. When they first came to America they scrubbed floors together. They'd meet in the middle and kiss. I don't know why but I thought that was very romantic. Then one day someone told her he was cavorting with a woman in Atlantic City. She didn't even let him pack. Her heart was still broken, she said, and she fell asleep crying. I kept waking up. I had to go to the toilet. I tiptoed in the dark. I didn't even flush. I was terrified I'd disturb her. The third or fourth time I smelled a bad smell. Like something spoiled or rotten. The fifth time I turned on the light. The toilet bowl was filled with blood. And lumps of stringy fibers. Like liver. Pieces of raw liver. From the butcher. I was so sleepy. The doctor had given me something to sleep. Why was liver coming out of me? And this awful smell? I went back to her bed. I had to go to the toilet again. And again. By morning I must have been close to death. She demanded her tea in bed. I pulled myself to the kitchen. I fell on the floor in a heap. What must have saved me was the kettle whistling. I couldn't reach up to turn it off. Where's my tea? What's wrong with you, girl? You can't even make my tea. I woke up in a hospital. I'd had a miscarriage. So you see how much I wanted you. Can't you? Can't you see how much I want you? (*Clutching* ALEXANDER *physically.*)

ALEXANDER: Momma, don't. I'm beginning to feel really unhappy.

RENA: Can't you see?

ALEXANDER: (*Breaking away from her.*) It comes out of nowhere.

NED: I get scared.

RENA: Can't you see?

(ALEXANDER *runs away from her.* RENA *has no arms to go to but* NED*'s; he accepts her reluctantly.*)

NED: Don't cry, Momma. (*In* ALEXANDER*'s direction.*) Come back!

RENA: (*Clutching* NED.) You're leaving me. What am I supposed to do?

(BENJAMIN *enters; he doesn't like what he sees.* RENA *quickly relinquishes* NED.)

BENJAMIN: Hi, Mom.

RENA: I made your favorites. Remember when you were captain of the football team and drank three quarts of milk every meal?

BENJAMIN: I'm not on any team anymore. (*To* ALEXANDER.) Lemon, come help me.

(BENJAMIN *and* ALEXANDER *go off.* NED *returns to bed; he's not feeling well. Several yellow lights go on. The soft bell rings. He presses his buzzer.*)

RENA: (*Alone.*) Aren't you glad to see me?

(RENA *sits on the swing. After a moment,* RICHARD *enters.*)

RENA: Your other son has arrived.

RICHARD: I hate using everyone's toilet.

RENA: Year after year, you're the one who insists on coming back here to Mrs. Pennington's. We could go to that place in New Hampshire Manny and Teresa rave about. You even told me to send for a brochure. I've never been to Europe.

RICHARD: I've been to Europe. Leon and I tried to find where Pop was born. We couldn't find it. I like it here. Except for the toilet. (*Angry.*) We can't afford Europe, for Christ's sake!

RENA: I can dream! Let's have a nice time.

RICHARD: I didn't come here not to have a nice time. Why couldn't he have turned out like Ben?

RENA: You want another Ben? A son who never comes home. Who never writes except when he wants something. This is the first time the family has been together in years. I should've bought flowers. I wonder why he's come.

RICHARD: Come here.

RENA: What do you want?

RICHARD: (*As she sits beside him.*) You're a good egg. It hasn't been easy for you.

RENA: Why are you talking like this all of a sudden?

RICHARD: I'm just trying to be nice.

RENA: I don't even recognize it anymore.

RICHARD: You wanted more.

RENA: Everybody wants more.

RICHARD: I've always been crazy about you.

RENA: What's wrong with wanting more?

(NED *presses the buzzer more urgently.*)

RICHARD: Things will be better soon. Four more years and we'll have nothing to spend money on but ourselves.

RENA: Just the two of us again.

RICHARD: It will be better. We'll move back here for good.

RENA: You've never stopped loving me for one minute, have you?

RICHARD: No, Mommy, I haven't. And I never shall.

RENA: Richard, they're both gone now. I want to go out on my own now, too.

RICHARD: Don't start those dumb, stupid, asinine threats one more time!

(BENJAMIN *and* ALEXANDER *enter, carrying a tennis racket, books, a suitcase.*)

BENJAMIN: You could show a little more enthusiasm.

ALEXANDER: (*Offering his hand.*) Congratulations, Benjamin. I hope you'll be very happy.

(*But* BENJAMIN'*s hands are full.*)

RICHARD: Hey, son!

BENJAMIN: Who won?

RICHARD: We slaughtered you. Yankees ten, Red Sox two.

BENJAMIN: We're still ahead in the series.

(HANNIMAN *runs in.*)

NED: I'm boiling! I feel like I'm going to explode!

(*She feels him, then quickly checks the monitoring devices.*)

RENA: (*Trying to kiss* BENJAMIN *hello.*) Tell me all about Yale. I want to know everything so I can be proud. What's your thesis on?

BENJAMIN: Ma, I've told you a dozen times.

RENA: Tell me again.

ALEXANDER: Twentieth Century Negro Poets.

(HANNIMAN *leaves quickly.*)

RENA: Isn't that fascinating.

RICHARD: Studying all that literature stuff is crap!

RENA: Don't be such a philistine!

BENJAMIN: It's my money and my education and my life.

(HANNIMAN *returns with* DR. DELLA VIDA. NED *begins to convulse slightly.*)

TONY: (*Checking the computer, then* NED.) He's going into shock! (*Turns off the machinery.*)

(HANNIMAN *hands him a huge syringe, which he injects into* NED's *groin or neck.*)

ALEXANDER: Benjamin doesn't want to go to law school. He wants to be a teacher or a writer. He wants to help people. Ned, what are they doing to you?

BENJAMIN: I'll be all right, Lemon. Law is helping people, too.

ALEXANDER: That's not what you told me! Ned, what's wrong? Why aren't you answering?

RICHARD: (*To* BENJAMIN.) Listen, mister smart ass big guy, don't make it sound like such a holy sacrifice! I got you this far. I got both of you this far. I got all of us this far.

RENA: Stop it, stop it, stop it!

ALEXANDER: *NED!*

RICHARD: You and your ungrateful prick of a brother!

RENA: We are not going to fight!

ALEXANDER: Why do you bring us back to this stupid place every year anyway? Just so we can feel poor? Benjamin is going to marry a rich girl he doesn't even love!

RENA: You're getting married?

RICHARD: Hey, I always say it's just as easy to marry a rich one.

BENJAMIN: You promised me you'd keep your mouth shut. Let's go for a swim. (*Throws* ALEXANDER *his suit.*)

RENA: Don't go. It's getting dark.

BENJAMIN: (*Gets his own suit.*) Fast!

RENA: It's too dark. Wait until tomorrow. I'll go with you.

RICHARD: (*Grabbing* ALEXANDER *as he starts out.*) Every time I look at you, every single time I see you, I wish to Christ your mother'd had that abortion!

RENA: (*A wail.*) NOOOOOO!

RICHARD: She wouldn't have another one. And I've been paying for it ever since.

RENA: I beg you!

ALEXANDER: Ned, help me! Where are you?

(NED *tries to get up, but is restrained by* DR. DELLA VIDA.)

(BENJAMIN *physically lifts* ALEXANDER *away from* RICHARD *and they start out.* RICHARD *grabs* RENA, *who is also leaving.*)

I'm going to be sick. (*Runs to sink.*)

TONY: It's okay, Ned. We're going to get through this.

RICHARD: Where do you think you're going? We can't afford another child, Rene. He'll just take all our pleasure away. All our money and all our hope.

RENA: Let go of me, Richard.

RICHARD: Listen to me, Rene. It's the Depression.

RENA: This time I mean it. This time I'm going for good.

(RICHARD *restrains her from leaving.*)

I only came back because you begged me! What else could I do? A woman can't get a decent job to use her brain. I had to sell lace and pins at Macy's for twelve dollars a week. I lost my chance with Drew Keenlymore.

RICHARD: We're back to him again? Miss Flirt! Miss Goddamn Flirt!

BENJAMIN: (*helping* ALEXANDER *at the sink.*) Lemon, are you all right?

ALEXANDER: Please don't call me Lemon anymore.

RICHARD: What does anyone know about not taking it anymore? Spending each day of my life at a job I hate, with people who don't know how smart I am.

BENJAMIN: Come on.

ALEXANDER: I can't throw up.

RICHARD: Not seeing my sons turn into anything I want as my sons—the one I love never at home, the other one always at home, to remind me of what a sissy's come out of my loving you. Don't leave me, Rene!

RENA: I am, I am. Let me go!

(RICHARD *is trying to hold a woman who doesn't want to be held. He hits her. She screams.*)

RICHARD: I don't want to live without you!

RENA: I'm supposed to stay here? For the rest of my life?

(RENA *breaks loose and runs off.* BENJAMIN *runs after her.* RICHARD *yanks* ALEXANDER *away from the sink and hurls him to the floor, falling on top of him, pinioning him beneath him and letting out all his venom and fury on his younger son.*)

RICHARD: You were a mistake! I didn't want you! I never wanted you! I should have shot my load in the toilet!

ALEXANDER: Mommy!

NED: (*Screaming out.*) Ben!

(BENJAMIN *runs back in. He somehow separates his father from his brother. He carries* ALEXANDER *off in his arms.*)

BENJAMIN: It's too late. There's nothing we can do. I shouldn't have come.

(RICHARD *pulls himself up off the floor. He doesn't know which way to go. He stumbles first in one direction, then in another, finally going off.*)

NED: It's too late. There's nothing we can do. I shouldn't have come.

HANNIMAN: Why, we're just starting.

TONY: You just had a little imbalance. It's a good sign. It means we're knocking out more of your infected cells than we expected. I think we just may be seeing some progress.

NED: That was awful. You sure it's not just poison? Would you tell me it's working, even when it's killing me? Did anyone anywhere in the entire history of the world have a happy childhood?

TONY: I'm sure George Bush was a very happy child.

HANNIMAN and NED: He still is.

(*They all smile.* TONY *turns the switch to the equipment on again and leaves.* HANNIMAN *wipes* NED's *damp brow.*)

NED: In eighteenth-century Holland—a country and culture that had never acted this way—there was a hysterical uprising against gays that resulted in the most awful witch hunts. Young boys were condemned, persecuted, throttled, executed . . . a fourteen-year-old boy was found guilty and drowned with a two-hundred-pound weight. Who was that kid? What was his name? What could he possibly ever have done to deserve such punishment, and in a Christian land?

Centuries later, historians, searching for a reason, discovered that, when all that happened, the sea walls along the Dutch coast were collapsing because of massive, unrelenting pressure from floods, accompanied by a plague of very hungry pile worms consuming the foundations.

The people, in that perverse cause-and-effect way that never seems to stop, had blamed the destruction of their coastline and its fortifications on the gay kids. God would inundate their Republic until it was punished and penance was paid to relieve the wrath of the Almighty.

When I was a little boy I thought colored girls were much sexier than white girls.

HANNIMAN: What happened?

NED: Boys. Any color. How did you meet Tony?

HANNIMAN: I was head nurse of this division when he was appointed director.

NED: Was it love at first sight?

HANNIMAN: None of your business.

NED: You don't seem very happy. Is it because he's such a ... Republican?

HANNIMAN: You think anyone black has anything to be happy about?

NED: It seems more personal.

HANNIMAN: Everyone in this entire hospital in every room on every floor is dying from something. They all come here to be saved. This is the new Lourdes. Congress gives us nine billion dollars a year to perform miracles. And God's a bit slow these days in the miracle department. You don't think that's enough to get you down?

NED: Still not personal enough.

HANNIMAN: You always say just what you want to?

NED: Pretty much. No matter what you say, x number of people are going to approve and x number aren't. You might as well say what you want to.

HANNIMAN: You obviously don't work for the government.

NED: So marrying a white man didn't solve any of your problems?

HANNIMAN: Did not marrying a colored girl solve any of yours? (*Starts to leave.*)

NED: Hey! I thought we were seeing some progress!

HANNIMAN: We are. (*Leaves.*)

ALEXANDER: (*Entering his Yale room, dressed most collegiately.*) The first thing upon entering a new life is to change one's name.

BEN: (*Entering with brownies and milk, wearing a* Y *athletic sweater.*) Ned?

ALEXANDER: Ben?

BEN: But Ben is logically the nickname for Benjamin.

ALEXANDER: I read this play called *Holiday* where there's a Ned. It could be a nickname for Alexander. It sounds very fresh and spiffy, don't you think? Ned. She still makes a good brownie.

BEN: (*Noticing some papers.*) What kind of dreadful way is this to start out? What happened?

ALEXANDER: What happened? I'm flunking psychology. And astronomy. And geology. And German. So far. What do I do?

BEN: Study.

ALEXANDER: That's very helpful. What did you win that letter for?

BEN: This one? Boxing, I think.

ALEXANDER: Boxing. Football. Squash. Tennis. Dean's List. Phi Bete. A after A after A. Prom committees, elected offices, scholarships, friends, girls ... You have done your parents and your alma mater and your country proud. You're even marrying a rich girl.

BEN: It's time to get married.

ALEXANDER: Do you love her yet?

BEN: She's as good as anyone.

ALEXANDER: What kind of dreadful way is this to start out? I don't want to be a lawyer.

BEN: Nobody's asked you to be a lawyer.

ALEXANDER: I always dreamed we'd be partners in something.

BEN: Why aren't you going to Europe with Theo?

ALEXANDER: Boy, is *Moby Dick* a bitch to get excited about. Are you sorry Pop made you go to law school?

BEN: I don't believe anybody makes you do anything you don't really want to.

ALEXANDER: That's good to know.

BEN: Why aren't you going to Europe this summer with Theo all expenses paid? It sounded like a wonderful offer.

(NED *has left his bed and moved closer to* ALEXANDER.)

NED: This is one of those moments in life we talked about. Would life be otherwise if you did or didn't do something differently? You're about to tell your brother ... something both painful and precious, something you don't understand, something you need help with. You want him to understand. Oh, how you want him to understand! He's not going to understand.

ALEXANDER: Will it be better if I don't tell him?

NED: I've always thought it would have been. I don't know. Why do you have to tell him at all?

ALEXANDER: Why not? Is it something so awful?

NED: (*Helplessly.*) But Ben is going to . . .

ALEXANDER: Going to what?

NED: (*Feebly.*) Make you . . .

ALEXANDER: Make me what?

NED: Make you do something I'd rather not have done. Just yet. They didn't know enough then!

ALEXANDER: How much do they know now! In my limited experience, so far as I can see, you don't have a very good record on just about anything concerning me. Or yourself. Why are you even here? Why are you letting them do all this to you? Do you trust that doctor? I don't. He's much too gorgeous. (*To* BEN.) We were lovers.

BEN: We were what!

ALEXANDER: Me and Theo!

NED: And so the journey begins. Do you feel any better?

BEN: Did he ask you?

ALEXANDER: (*To* BEN.) Yes. (*To* NED.) Yes!

BEN: He shouldn't have done that.

ALEXANDER: Oh, I wanted to do it.

BEN: How can you be so certain of that?

ALEXANDER: I don't believe anybody makes you do anything you don't really want to.

BEN: This is about you, not me. Sometimes we do things we don't want to.

ALEXANDER: Like become a lawyer and get married to someone you don't love?

BEN: Look, Sara and I are just getting started, and, listen, get off my case. What happened with Theo?

ALEXANDER: We made love. Right here. I went to Theo and asked him: I'm flunking out of your German class, could I do something for extra credit, and we went out and drank beer, and we came back here, and he asked me: would you like to make love, and I walked to this door, and opened it, and said: I think you'd better go, and I closed the door, and ran right back into his arms. And I passed.

BEN: I believe this is something they now think they can change.

ALEXANDER: It felt wonderful!

BEN: It's unhealthy, it's caused by something unhealthy, it'll do nothing but make you unhappy.

NED: How are all the men in my family such experts in these matters?

BEN: Everybody knows.

NED: Everybody does not know! Everybody is told!

BEN: What's the difference?

ALEXANDER: Unhealthy? (BEN *nods.*) Caused by something?

BEN: A possessive mother. An absent father.

NED: That's what they thought then.

ALEXANDER: Absent? Richard was always there. That was the problem. Possessive doesn't sound precise enough for Rena. (*To* NED.) Where do I get more up-to-date information?

BEN: You see a psychiatrist.

ALEXANDER: See him do what?

BEN: You talk to him.

ALEXANDER: Talk to *him*?

BEN: About this.

ALEXANDER: I'm talking to you.

BEN: What do you expect me to say?

ALEXANDER: "I don't care if you've got purple spots, I love you." Theo said there are lots of us. We can tell each other like Jewish people can.

BEN: Horseshit!

ALEXANDER: *We* mustn't fight, Benjamin.

NED: Why not? If you don't agree, fight, Alexander. Fight back! Never run away from a fight.

ALEXANDER: Which one of you am I supposed to fight? It's like Richard and Rena—each one is pulling so hard in opposite directions I'm being torn in two. (*To* NED.) Please call me Ned.

(*To* BEN.) So you do think I'm sick? (*No answer.*) You do. I told Theo that going to Europe as his assistant on his Guggenheim was a terrific opportunity but that after walking round and around the block all night long I decided not to go.

BEN: Good man.

ALEXANDER: I told him no because I don't love him.

BEN: You told him no because you know it's wrong.

NED: (*To* BEN.) I told him no because . . . because I knew you wanted me to tell him no.

BEN: (*To* NED.) You told him no because you knew it was considered wrong and unhealthy and sick.

ALEXANDER: Don't I just not love Theo because I just don't love Theo?

BEN: There's something called psychoanalysis. It's the latest thing. You lie down on a couch every day and say whatever comes into your head.

NED: (*As* ALEXANDER *looks at him, suddenly worried.*) Why listen to me? I can only predict epidemics and plagues.

ALEXANDER: What have I done?

NED: You're letting Ben push you on to a treadmill of revolving doctors, not one of whom will know a fucking thing about what makes *your* heart tick.

ALEXANDER: What will they do to me?

NED: They will turn you into a productive human being.

ALEXANDER: What's wrong with that? I'm flunking every course.

NED: While they teach you to love yourself they will also teach you to hate your heart. It's their one great trick. All these old Jewish doctors—the sons of Sigmund—exiled from their homelands, running from Hitler's death camps, for some queer reason celebrated their freedom on our shores by deciding to eliminate homosexuals. That's what you are. It's going to be a long time before you can say the word out loud. Over and over and over again they will pound into your consciousness through constant repetition: you're sick, you're sick, you're sick. So your heart is going to lie alone. So you see, you should have gone to Europe with Theo.

ALEXANDER: Ben—I'm scared.

BEN: You're making all the right decisions. I'll always fight for you and defend you and protect you. All I ask is that you try. The talking cure, it's called. (*Puts his arm around* ALEXANDER'S *shoulder.*)

ALEXANDER: Talking? I should be cured real fast. (*Leaving with* BEN.) Theo gave me crabs. Do you know what crabs are? (BEN *nods.*) I didn't but I do now.

(*They exit.* HANNIMAN *enters with her cart. Sounds of chanting outside can be dimly heard.*)

HANNIMAN: We need more blood.

NED: What are you opening, a store? Do you know how many blood tests I've had in the past twelve years? It's definitely a growth industry. The tyranny of the blood test. Ladies and gentlemen, step right up and watch the truth drawn right before your very eyes. We are being tested for the presence of a virus that may or may not be the killer. We are being tested to discover if this and/or that miraculous new discovery that may or may not kill the virus which may or may not be the killer is working. We live in constant terror that the number of healthy cells, which may or may not be an accurate indicator of anything at all and which the virus that may or may not be the killer may or may not be destroying, will decline and fall. What does any of this *mean*? Before each blood test, no one sleeps. (*Singing.*) "Nessun dorma." Awaiting each result, the same. The final moments are agony. On a piece of paper crowded with computerized chitchat that, depending on whom you ask, is open to at least two and often more contradictory interpretations, and which your doctor is holding in his hand, is printed the latest clairvoyance of your life expectancy. May I have the winning envelope, please?

HANNIMAN: Boy, you are one piece of cake. What happened between you and your people out there?

NED: You ran out of miracles.

HANNIMAN: Not personal enough.

NED: They look to me for leadership and I don't know how to guide them. I'm going to die and they're going to die, only they're nineteen and twenty-four and somehow born into this world and I feel so fucking guilty that I've failed them. I wanted to be Moses but I only could be Cassandra.

HANNIMAN: And you lay all that on yourself?

NED: Why not?

HANNIMAN: If people don't want to be led, they don't want to be led. You're not as grand and important as you think you are.

NED: In a few more years more Africans will be dying from this plague than are being born. If this stuff works, only rich white men will get it. I call that genocide. What do you call it? How do you go to sleep at night lying beside your husband knowing all that? What are you doing for *your* people out there?

HANNIMAN: I don't have to take this shit. (*Walks out.*)

NED: (*Calling after her.*) You're as grand and important as you want to be!

(*Loud banging is heard, then* BEN'*s voice.*)

BEN: Ned! Your landlady says you're in there! Open up. Open up the goddamned door! Alexander!

(BEN *is banging on the door of a sparsely furnished New York studio apartment.* ALEXANDER *sits staring into space.* BEN *finally breaks the door down. He carries a bottle of champagne.*)

You haven't been to work in a week. Your office said you were home sick. Why don't you answer the phone? Does Dr. . . . I can't remember the new one's name . . . know you're like this? Ned, come on, talk to me. You always talk to me. Ned, God damn it, please answer me! You know, you're not a very good uncle. You never come and see my kids. Alexandra would like to see her namesake. Timmy wants to know all about the movie business. Betsy—sometimes I think my feelings for my firstborn are unnatural. Have you been staring into space for a week? Come on—congratulations! You're going to London!

Your career is progressing nicely. Are you going to talk to me?

(BEN *uncorks the champagne.* NED *gives him a cup.* BEN *pours some and offers it to* ALEXANDER, *who refuses.*)

ALEXANDER: Be careful you don't ever give me one of your secrets.

NED: I told you not to tell him.

ALEXANDER: Fuck you! (*Mimicking.*) "I told you this!" "I told you that!" I've had enough of your ... lack of cooperation.

NED: Well, tough shit and fuck you yourself, you little parasite.

ALEXANDER: Parasite?

NED: Bloodsucker. Leech. Hanger-on. Freeloader. You're like the very virus itself and I can't get rid of you.

ALEXANDER: I didn't know that's what you wanted to do.

NED: There's never been a virus that's been successfully eradicated.

ALEXANDER: (*Repeating.*) I didn't know that's what you wanted to do.

BEN: Who is it this time?

(BEN *offers him the cup of champagne again. This time* ALEXANDER *takes it.* BEN *drinks out of the bottle.*)

ALEXANDER: Six shrinks later I'm still the most talkative one in class. When do I graduate? You always take care of me. Why? (*No answer.*) Why?

BEN: Tell me about him.

ALEXANDER: Which one?

BEN: Any one.

ALEXANDER: Dr. Schwartz kept calling me a pervert. Dr. Grossman said I was violating God's laws by not fathering children. Dr. Nussbaum was also very uncomplimentary. I ran into him getting fucked in the Provincetown dunes. Dr. . . . I go to all the doctors you send me to. One doesn't do the trick, you find me another.

BEN: What's wrong!

ALEXANDER: I didn't know life could be so lonely.

BEN: I'm sorry. You'll meet someone.

ALEXANDER: Oh, that. I already tried that. Hundreds of times. At first I wanted love back. But now I'm willing to give that up if someone would just stay put and let me love him. That's really a person who likes himself a lot, huh?

BEN: Don't give up. Your self-pity will . . . diminish.

ALEXANDER: I did meet someone. He loved every book I loved. Every symphony and pop song and junk food. I couldn't believe this man was interested in me. He was so . . . beautiful. Beauty rarely looks at me. I couldn't stop feeling his skin, touching his face. (*Pointing to mattress.*) Right there. There! All night long, two days through, we couldn't let go of each other.

And then came the brainwashing session. What did that mind-bender say to turn me into such a monster? I walked home very slowly. I came in here. Peter had made breakfast. Nobody ever made me breakfast. He smiled and said, "I've missed you." He missed me. "We have one more day before I have to go back." He was finishing his doctorate at Harvard. The perfect man for *anyone* to take home to the folks. And I said . . . I actually said . . . I don't know where the words came from or how I could say them . . . but I said: "You have to leave now." God damn you!

BEN: Me?

ALEXANDER: They're your witch doctors! (*To* NED.) All this psychoanalysis shit and you're what I've got to show for it?

NED: I did not send you into psychoanalysis.

ALEXANDER: Stop trying to keep your hands so fucking clean! *You're* the bloodsucker!

BEN: Ned . . . ?

ALEXANDER: Why do I go to them? One after another. One doesn't do the trick: step right up, your turn at bat. Why do I listen to them? Why do I listen to you? How do we still love each other, when all we do is . . . this? Peter could be here (*Holding out his empty arms.*) right now. Why are you so insistent? Why do I obey you? You don't put a gun to my head. Why don't I say: get out of my life, I'll make my own rules? I could be loved! But you do put a gun to my head. You won't love me unless I change. Well, it's too powerful a force to change! It's got to be a part of me! It doesn't want to die. And fights tenaciously to stay alive, against all odds. And no matter what anyone does to try and kill it. Why don't you just leave me alone? We don't have to see each other. Are you afraid to let go of me, too? Why? Why am I—why are we both—such collaborators? And how can I love you when part of me thinks you're murdering me?

BEN: You're very strange. You just lay it all right out there. You always have.

NED: (*To* BEN.) Answer him!

BEN: What do you want me to say! (*Pause.*) Change is hard.

ALEXANDER: How about grief? And sadness. And mourning for lost life and love and what might have been.

BEN: Try not to be so melodramatic.

ALEXANDER: Melodramatic? Who are you? Do I know you? Sometimes you can be a very mysterious person.

BEN: I've heard excellent things about another doctor. In London.

ALEXANDER: Why'd you stay away from home so much? (*No answer.*) Why'd you stay away from home? (*No answer.*) Why did you run away?

BEN: I didn't run away.

ALEXANDER: You were never there.

NED: Answer him!

BEN: (*After a long pause.*) I didn't have a mother.

ALEXANDER: You never had a *mother*?

BEN: You asked me why I never came home. That's why I never came home.

ALEXANDER: You thought Rena didn't love you?

BEN: She doesn't.

ALEXANDER: Mommy doesn't love you? (*To* NED.) Did you know this?

NED: That's what he believes.

BEN: She was never there! She had so many jobs. She was always out taking care of everyone in the entire world except me. So I went out and did a thousand projects at a time because I thought that was how I'd get my mother's love. If I got *another* A or headed up *another* organization, she'd notice me and pay attention to me and I'd win some approval from her. I needed her and she wasn't there and I resent it bitterly. (*Long pause.*) And I'll never forgive her for that.

ALEXANDER: (*Shaken, feeling he must defend her.*) She had to work! Pop didn't make enough! She was doing her best.

BEN: That's all she cares about. *Her* best. She *made* Daddy quit working for Uncle Leon. It was a good job. All through the Depression, Leon was rich. Pop had been making big bucks. Suddenly he's no longer the breadwinner, with no self-respect. He was out of work for something like seven, eight years before the war finally came and there was work in Washington for everybody. So we moved to Washington where he made ten times less than he'd made with Leon.

ALEXANDER: You can't blame that on her!

BEN: Why not! She had to be the star. She never stopped. She had a million jobs. She had a few spare hours she ran over to take dictation from a couple of bozos who repaired wrecked trucks. Leon found Pop a job as American counsel in the Virgin Islands. A big house, servants, tax-free salary. A fortune in those days. They turned it down.

ALEXANDER: She said there wasn't any milk for babies. You were just born.

BEN: You boil milk. You use powdered. What did all the tens of thousands of babies born there drink? Have you heard about any mass demise of Virgin Island babies? She didn't want to go! She felt so "useful." And so he stayed home, unemployed, playing pinochle with the boys.

ALEXANDER: Why didn't he hustle his ass like she did?

BEN: You're not listening to me. She took his balls away! Why are you defending her so? She almost smothered you to death.

ALEXANDER: She was the only one interested in me!

BEN: Interested in you? What did she ever do to help you develop one single ability or interest or gift you ever had? You wanted to act, sing, dance, write, create ... whatever. That's what parents are supposed to do! Richard crucified every single one of those desires and she stood by and let him. All she does is talk endlessly and forever about herself!

ALEXANDER: It wasn't her. It wasn't! It was him. It was all him. It was Richard. Why aren't you mad at him for being so weak instead of her for trying to be strong?

BEN: She called all the shots and she called them from her own selfish point of view.

ALEXANDER: You don't like her as much as I don't like him. What happens when a kid is chosen for the wrong team? It's as if we each took one parent for our very own. And each of them chose one of us. The whole procedure had nothing to do with love. Can you say "I love you?" Out loud? To anyone? And mean it? (*No answer. To* NED.) Can you? (*No answer.*)

BEN: There's just an anger inside me that never goes away. I've got to get out of here. I'm late. Walk me back to the office.

ALEXANDER: How'd you figure all this out? (*No answer.*) You have just told me I shouldn't love my mother. How did you figure this all out!

BEN: (*Another long pause.*) I'm being psychoanalyzed.

ALEXANDER: (*Pause.*) I don't know why but that scares the shit out of me.

BEN: It should make you feel better you're not the only one.

ALEXANDER: It's all the decisions I let you make for me because you were the only one. What happened? God, wouldn't it be wonderful if it were another man.

BEN: You know how Richard always yelled at you, no matter what you did, you couldn't do anything right? That's how Sara treats Timmy. She says I . . . I withhold. I don't show how I feel toward anyone and that makes her overreact and overreach and vent her anger on young Timmy. My son . . . he . . . she . . . she's so hard on him, she takes everything out on him that's meant for me. I called her . . . a controlling bitch. She says she can't stop herself from doing it. Alexander, it's a mess. The poor kid's got some kind of stomach ulceration now. He'll suddenly start bleeding, he can never be out of range of a toilet, and he's only a kid, he'll have this all his life. He's such a good kid. He came into my room and started crying. I want him to be smart in school and the kid just isn't. And he knows it disappoints the shit out of me. Ned, why doesn't he do better? He's smart. I just know it! He was crying. He started screaming I didn't love him. And I'd never loved him. Why are you looking at me that way? We're working on it! Sara's in therapy, too. She's learning. I'm learning. Richard and Rena couldn't learn. We can learn. We mustn't stop trying to learn.

NED: "And the sins of the fathers shall visit unto the third and fourth generations."

BEN: No! I don't believe that! We *can* change it!

NED: And all those years you told me it was worse for me and I believed you!

BEN: It was. It was worse for you.

NED: No, it wasn't. Why was it so important for you to hold on to that? Why was it so important to you to make me the sick one? Were you so angry at Rena that you had to make my homosexuality so awful just to blame her? It wasn't so hot for either of us! It made you stay away from home. And it didn't make me gay. It made both of us have a great deal of difficulty saying "I love you."

BEN: Ned—go and call Peter back.

ALEXANDER: Thank you, Ben. I called Peter back. I asked him to meet me. Which he did. At the Savoy Plaza. I took this grand suite and ordered filet mignon and champagne and flowers, tons of flowers. I apologized over and over again for what I had done. He said he recalled our time together as very pleasant. I practically pounced on him and threw him on the bed and held him in my arms and kissed him all over. He told me he was very happily in love with someone else and he thought it best that he leave. Which he did.

BEN: I'm sorry. I have to get back to the office. I really am sorry. I have a meeting. Good luck in London. Maybe you'll meet someone.

ALEXANDER: Are you saying loving a man is now okay?

BEN: Keep fighting. Keep on fighting. Don't give up. The answers will present themselves. They really will. For both of us!

(*They go off.*)

NED: I haven't been honest with you. I left out the hardest part for me to talk about. It was done by another Ned, someone inside of me who took possession of me and did something I've been terrified, every day of my life ever since, he might come back and do again. And, this time, succeed. After my father beat me and Mom up and told me he'd never wanted me and after I told my brother I was gay and after my brother got married and before my first year's final exams that I knew I'd flunk, I pulled a bottle of some kind of pills which belonged to my roommate whose father was a doctor out of his bureau drawer and swallowed them all. I had wanted to take a knife and slice a foot or arm off. I had wanted to see blood, gushing everywhere, making a huge mess, and floating me away on its sea. But there were only pills. I'm only going to take two for a headache and two more to help me sleep. I have finals on Monday and there's no way I can pass. Where else can I go? Back to Eden Heights? I'd rather be dead. So where? Every social structure I'm supposed to be a part of—my family, my religion, my school, my friends, my neighborhood, my work, my city, my state, my country, my government, my newspaper, my television—tells me over and over what I feel and see and think and do is sick. The only safe place left is the dark. I want to go to sleep. It's Friday. I want to sleep till Tuesday. (*Swallowing* HANNIMAN'*s pills with* BEN'*s champagne.*) This couple of pills will take me till tomorrow and these until Sunday and ... Monday ... now I can sleep till Tuesday. Might as well take a few more. Just in case. Pop's right, of course. I'm a failure. (*Looking at himself in the mirror over the sink.*) You even look like Richard. You'll look like him for the rest of your life. I am more my father's child than ever I wanted to be. I've fought so hard not to look like you. I've fought so hard not to inherit your failure. Poor newly named Ned. Trying so hard to fight failure. Now increasing at an awful rate. I woke up in the hospital and Ben was there beside me.

ALEXANDER'S VOICE: Help! I'm drowning! Don't let me drown!

NED: That night at Mrs. Pennington's when Benjamin stopped Poppa from beating me up, he put me on his shoulders and carried me down to the shore. We swam and played and ducked under each other's arms and legs. We lay on the big raft, way out on the Sound, side by side, not saying a word, looking at the stars. I held his hand. He said, Come dive with me. I dived in after he did and I got caught under the raft and I couldn't get out from under. I thrashed desperately this way and that and I had no more breath.

ALEXANDER'S VOICE: Help! I'm drowning! Don't let me drown!

NED: When I thought I would surely die, he rescued me and saved me, Benjamin did.

(BENJAMIN *carries in a limp* ALEXANDER *and lays him on the ground. Both are wet from the ocean.*)

He got me to the shore and he laid me out on the sand and he pressed my stomach so the poison came out and he kissed me on the lips so I might breathe again.

TONY: (*Entering.*) Ned, I've run the tests. The new genes are adhering. We're halfway there. We can go on with the final part. Say "Thank you." Say "Congratulations." You begged for a few more years. I may have bought you life. (*Leaves.*)

NED: Okay, Ned—he happy. Be exuberant! You're halfway there. (*Singing.*) "Hold my hand and we're halfway there, Hold my hand and I'll take you there. Someday. Somewhere. Somehow . . ."

End of Act Two

Act Three

(HANNIMAN *removes three more sacks of blood from the small insulated chest on her cart and inserts them into the wall machine.* DR. DELLA VIDA, *wearing the white dress uniform of a Public Health Service officer, checks that everything is in readiness.* NED, *wearing a navy blue robe with a red ribbon on the lapel, looks out the window.*)

NED: Three hundred and seventy arrests and not one lousy reporter or camera so no one sees it but a couple hundred of your scientists with nothing better to do than look out their windows because their microscopes are constipated.

TONY: I thought your soapbox was in retirement.

NED: You bought me life.

TONY: Nice robe.

NED: Navy blue and red. The smart colors Felix always called them.

(TONY *wheels in from the outside hallway a new machine—the Ex-Cell-Aerator, another elaborate invention, replete with its own dials and switches and tubings and lights.*)

What's that?

TONY: (*Proudly.*) I call it the Ex-Cell-Aerator. Your reassembled blood will be pumped through it so it can be exposed to particles of—

NED: That's it? I thought it was the other one.

TONY: It's both of them.

NED: It takes two? Did you dream all this up?

TONY: I try to be as creative as the law allows.

NED: (*Re: the sacks of blood.*) The little buggers went and multiplied.

TONY: Enriched. They got enriched. Hey, don't touch those.

NED: Do genes get loose and act uncontrollably, like viruses?

TONY: You bet. It's scary trying to modify nature.

NED: Despite everything I know and said and stood for, I have fucked with the enemy and he has given me hope.

TONY: I'm not your enemy.

NED: Why are you all dressed up?

TONY: The President wants to know all about this. (*Indicates that* NED *should get in bed.*)

NED: Any of my blood you want to slip him, hey . . . You're going to the White House!

TONY: Yes, I am. I go quite often.

NED: (*As* TONY *and* HANNIMAN *reconnect him to the wall tubing.*) Tell me . . . . you're a doctor, but you're also an officer in the service of your country. You're compelled to obey orders. How can research be legislated? You're an artist. How can you be free enough to create? It's like asking writers to write not using any vowels.

(HANNIMAN *leaves.*)

TONY: (*Connecting the Ex-Cell-Aerator to the wall apparatus.*) I run the premier research facility in the entire world. The American people are very lucky to have a place like this. And you got him all wrong. He's a good guy. He's got a heart. He really wants this disease to go away.

NED: He's brain-dead and you're brainwashed.

TONY: Lay off my wife, will you? Any fights you got with me, pick them with me. (*Hits a computer key to start everything going.*)

NED: Tony, all your top assistants are gay. What's that all about? When I bring down all my young men for meetings, you look at them so ... (*Can't find the word.*)

TONY: So what?

NED: You can't take your eyes off them.

TONY: It's very sad ... what's happening.

NED: Yes, it is. What kind of life do you want to he leading that you're not? Why is everyone down here afraid to call a plague a plague? Are you punishing us or yourself? (*Calling after him as he leaves.*) You get away with murder because you're real cute and everybody wants to go to bed with you! Nobody wanted to go to bed with Ed Koch. Him we could get rid of. (*Talking to the Ex-Cell-Aerator.*) You're the cure? I hope you come in a portable version, like a laptop. Can you find me a boyfriend while you're at it? Way to win the charm contest, Ned. You'll never get them in your arms that way. Mom, you said there wasn't anything in the world your son couldn't do.

(HANNIMAN *comes in and pulls a curtain around the bed.*

RENA, *now about seventy, sits in a hospital waiting area trying unsuccessfully to read some old magazines. Occasionally she gets up to look inside a room through an open door.*

After a moment, NED, *wearing an overcoat and carrying a suitcase, enters. They are strangely distant with each other. Sounds of baseball game on the TV.)*

RENA: (*To the unseen* RICHARD.) I'm closing this so I don't have to hear that ball game. (*Does so.*) When he sees you here he'll put two and two together and realize we sent for you.

NED: Doesn't he know?

RENA: Some things you don't want to know, even if you know. How's London? You never write to me.

NED: It's great. Very productive. Where's Ben?

RENA: They took a break. Sara's been wonderful. She hasn't left my side. So.

NED: You always wanted to travel.

RENA: He isn't dead yet.

NED: I'm just saying you've got something to look forward to.

RENA: How about giving me a chance to mourn first? Why are we talking like this to each other? I haven't seen you in six, seven years. Are you still going to a psychiatrist?

NED: I can go every day for seventy-five dollars a week.

RENA: That used to be three months' rent. How in God's name do you find enough to talk about every day?

NED: I fall asleep a lot.

RENA: You pay someone to fall asleep? You kids, you and your psychiatrists think you know it all. Then why aren't we perfect after all these years?

NED: Did you and Richard have a good sex life?

RENA: That's none of your business.

NED: I just thought I'd ask.

RENA: Well, don't.

NED: Did he want sex more than you, or did you want it and he wouldn't?

RENA: Stop it!

NED: You used to tell me everything.

RENA: Well, here's something I'm not going to. Our lives weren't about sex. Is sex what controls your life?

NED: I don't know. Why don't you try and look up Drew Keenlymore?

RENA: Why don't you try and stop being so fresh?

NED: Didn't you love him?

RENA: Why are you so obsessed with Drew Keenlymore?

NED: One should be able to have the man one loves.

RENA: Life should be a lot of things.

NED: Did he ever ask you to marry him? Did he?

RENA: I was invited to the Keenlymore private island estate in Western Canada for the entire summer. What does that tell you?

NED: But you didn't go.

RENA: He was ready to marry me. There! Does that make you happy?

NED: If you'd listened to your heart, and not been so afraid, that would have made me happy.

RENA: Listen to my heart. You've seen too many movies. Have you listened to your heart? I don't hear about any secret long-lost love you're keeping in a purse on the top shelf of your closet.

NED: I don't fall in love. People don't fall in love with me.

RENA: That's too bad.

NED: I want to love them. I want them to love me back.

RENA: Everyone should have someone.

NED: Kids are some sort of sum total of both their parents. We pick up a lot of traits from whatever kind of emotional subtext is going on.

RENA: I'm supposed to understand that mouthful of jargon?

NED: We've got both of you in us.

RENA: Are we getting blamed for all of this?

NED: I've just finally got the courage to say what I want to say.

RENA: I don't recall your ever being delinquent in that department. Well, I always tried to instill courage in you. But you can't always just say what you think.

NED: You saw how much Pop hated me. You must have had some sense that if you'd only left him, I wouldn't have had to go through all that shit.

RENA: Don't use that language. I tried to make up for it by loving you more.

NED: It doesn't work that way.

RENA: It would appear it doesn't.

NED: Why didn't you leave him for good?

RENA: You don't run away when things don't work out.

NED: You ran away from Drew.

RENA: Some courage I had and some courage I didn't have. I don't cry over spilt milk.

NED: Are you admitting you didn't love your husband?

RENA: I am not! You don't have so many choices as you seem to think!

NED: I'm homosexual. I would like you to accept that but I don't care if you don't, because I have.

RENA: You don't care? So I was a lousy mother.

NED: Don't do that.

RENA: Why not? You just said I was. Not very good value for all my years, is it? Some psychiatrist, some stranger, turns your son against you and declares me a bad mother.

NED: The preference now is to stay away from judgmental words like "good" or "bad."

RENA: Of course it's judgmental! Is this some kind of joke? You think any mother likes her son to be a . . . I'm not even going to say the word, that's how judgmental I think it is. I never criticized my parents. I worshiped the ground my mother walked on. I respected my father, even if he wasn't the most affectionate man in the world.

NED: Your father never smiled a day in his life.

RENA: Life was hard! They ran a tiny grocery store in a hostile neighborhood where neither of them spoke English and all the customers were Irish Catholics who hated us and never paid their bills. My parents didn't marry for love. They married to stay alive! Most kids grow up and leave home. You left home and found new parents called psychiatrists. I'm sorry the old ones were so disappointing. Sum total? Of both of us? You can also be so much more than that. I always told your father he should show his feelings more. He couldn't do it. He never would talk about his dreams. I don't even know what his dreams were. I guess they were taken away from him before I even knew him. He really did love you! I knew someday we'd reap the whirlwind. Why didn't Ben become one, too? He was there, too.

NED: I'm beginning to think it isn't caused by anything. I was born this way.

RENA: I don't believe that.

NED: I like being gay. It's taken me a very, very, very long time. I don't want to waste any more, tolerating your being ashamed of me, or anyone I care about being ashamed of me. If you can't accept that, you won't see your younger son again.

RENA: He has to die for you even to come home as it is. It makes you happy? Anything that makes you happy makes me happy. Miss Pollyanna, that's me. Go say hello to your father. Please don't tell him your wonderful news that makes you so happy.

(*She takes his suitcase from him and goes off.* NED *pulls the curtain around the bed, revealing* RICHARD *in it, half-asleep, with the ball game still on.* NED *comes in and turns the TV off.* RICHARD *wakes up.*)

RICHARD: Who won?

NED: Hi, Pop.

RICHARD: This is it, boy. I'm not going to make it.

NED: Sure you are.

RICHARD: I'm ready to go.

NED: Hey, I want you to see my first movie. I wrote it and produced it. It's good!

RICHARD: My goddamned Yankees can't break their losing streak. Ben's goddamned Red Sox may win the pennant.

NED: It cost two million dollars. I was paid a quarter of a million dollars.

RICHARD: Movies. The thee-ay-ter. When are you going to grow up?

NED: I've discovered how to make a living from it.

RICHARD: At least Ben listened to me. He's raking it in. He's senior partner over two hundred lawyers. Two million dollars. That's a hot one. I'm glad it's over. What's your name now?

NED: I've been Ned since I was eighteen.

RICHARD: Eighteen. That's when your mother started signing over her paychecks to your psychiatrist. I wouldn't have anything to do with it. She could have bought lots of nice clothes. She could have looked real pretty. I never felt good. I've felt sick all my life. In and out of doctors' offices and still the pain in my bloody gut. Nothing ever took it away. I never had a father either. So long, boy. (*He rolls over, with his back to* NED.)

NED: What do you mean, you never had a father either? (*No answer.*) Pop? Poppa? (RICHARD *doesn't answer.* NED *starts out . . .*)

RICHARD: My father was a mohel. You know what that is?

NED: The man who does the circumcision.

RICHARD: It was supposed to be a holy honor. God was supposed to bless him and his issue forever. One day he cut too much foreskin and this rich baby was mutilated for life. My mom and pop ran away and changed our name. Then Pop ran away. Forever.

NED: Mom said Grandma Sybil threw him out for sleeping with another woman in Atlantic City.

RICHARD: That's what she told people. He ran away when the kid he mutilated grew up and tracked him down. He couldn't have an erection without great pain and he was out for Pop's blood. I never told anyone. Not even your mother. I was afraid if I told her she wouldn't marry me. Maybe I should have told her. I wanted her more than she wanted me. I thought I could convince her and I never could. I helped my father. I was his assistant. All the time, the blood. Bawling babies terrified out of their wits. Tiny little cocks with pieces peeled off them. I had to dispose of the pieces. I buried them. He made me memorize all the Orthodox laws. If I made a mistake, he beat me. "You are forbidden to touch your membrum in self-gratification. You are forbidden to bring on an erection. It is forbidden to discharge semen in vain. Two bachelors must not sleep together. Two bachelors must not gaze upon each other. Two bachelors who lie down together and know each other and touch each other, it is equal to killing a person and saying blood is all over my hands. It is forbidden ... It is forbidden ..." He made me learn all that and then he ran away. I never stopped hating him. It's hard living with your gut filled with hate. Good luck to you, boy. Anything you want to say to me?

(RICHARD *rolls over and turns his back on him.* NED *stands there, trying to work up his courage to say what he has to say. Finally, finally, he does so.*)

NED: I'm sorry your life was a disappointment, Poppa. Poppa, you were cruel to me, Poppa.

(*There is no answer. He pulls the curtain closed again.*)

Poppa died. I didn't cry. My movie was a success. I made another. I realized how little pleasure achievement gave me. Slowly I became a writer. It suited me. I'd finally found a way to make myself heard. And "useful"—that word Rena so reveled in trumpeting. I would address the problems of my new world. Every gay man I knew was fucking himself to death. I wrote about that. Every gay man I knew wanted a lover. I wrote about that. I said that having so much sex made finding love impossible. I made my new world very angry. As

when I was a child, such defiance made me flourish. My writing and my notoriety prospered.

I stopped going to psychoanalysts. I'd analyzed, observed,
regurgitated, parsed, declined, X-rayed, and stared down
every action, memory, dream, recollection, thought, instinct,
and deed, from every angle I'd been able to come up with.

(NED *pulls back the curtain and gets into bed. He reconnects himself to
the tubing.*)

I spent many years looking for love—in the very manner I'd
criticized. How needy man is. And with good reason. When I
finally met someone, I was middle-aged. His name was Felix
Turner. Eleven months later he was sick and nineteen months
later he was dead. I had spent so many years looking for and
preparing for and waiting for Felix. Just as he came into my
arms and just as I was about to say "I love you, Felix," the
plague came along and killed him. And the further away I've
got from the love I had, the more I question I ever had it in
the first place.

Ben invested my money wisely and I am rich. When I get
angry with him for not joining me in fighting this plague, he
points out that he has made me financially independent so I
could afford to be an activist. Ben has made all the Weeks
family, including Rena and his children, rich. That's what
he wanted to do—indeed I believe that's been his mission in
life—to give all of us what he and I never had as children—
and he's accomplished it.

(BEN *stands in the Eden Heights apartment, smoking a cigar. Scat-
tered cartons and packing crates.*)

NED: Did you ever think you'd spend one more night in Eden Heights?

BEN: I consider it one of the greatest achievements of my life that I got out of here alive.

NED: Don't you ever stop and think how far we've come?

BEN: No. Never.

(RENA *is on the phone. She is now almost ninety.* BEN *sits in a chair and reads a business magazine.*)

RENA: (*Loudly.*) I'm coming home! I'll be there tomorrow! Back with all you dear chums I've loved since childhood! I can hardly wait! (*Hangs up.*) The woman's deaf. Paula's deaf and Nettie's moved to an old people's kibbutz in Israel and Belle is blind and Lydia's dead. Belle's husband brought you both into this world. Lydia introduced me to Richard. She didn't want him. (*Starts rummaging in a carton.*) All our past—in one battered carton from the Safeway. Aah, I'm going to throw it all away.

NED: No, I want it. It's our history.

RENA: Some history. So you can dredge up more unhappy memories to tell a psychiatrist how much you hated your father.

NED: (*To* BEN.) Don't you want to take anything for a memento?

BEN: You're the family historian. I leave the past to you.

NED: Your West Point letters, your yearbooks . . .

BEN: I've burned the mortgage. You're the one with the passion for remembering.

NED: Is that the way we handle it? I remember and you don't?

BEN: Maybe so. Maybe you've hit the nail on the head, young brother.

RENA: (*Comes across* RICHARD'*s watch chain.*) He was Phi Beta Kappa and Law Journal. He majored in Greek and Latin. They didn't let many Jews into Yale in those days. You would have thought he'd have done better.

NED: Both brothers such failures. Uncle Leon wound up broke, hanging around the Yale Club trying to bum loans off old Yalies. I could never understand why you paid for his funeral.

BEN: He wasn't such a bad guy.

RENA: Aunt Judith threw him out when she discovered all his bimbos.

BEN: Some old judge I met told me, "If only Leon had been castrated instead of circumcised, he'd have wound up on the Supreme Court."

RENA: I've lived in this room for over fifty years. We moved down here on a three-month temporary job. Some man had almost burned to death and they needed a new one fast. The poor chap died and the job was Richard's. (*Comes across the navy blue crocheted purse and pulls out the letters and tries to read them.*)

NED: Ah, the famous letters. (*Knows them by heart.*) "I find my schedule will perhaps bring me into the vicinity of New York on 4th May; might you be available for luncheon?"

RENA: That was at Delmonico's.

NED: "I find I must reschedule; will you be available instead on the 10th inst.?" "It now appears the 10th must be replaced by the

20th and even this is not firm." Why did I think they were so romantic?

RENA: They were romantic. They are romantic.

NED: Maybe you'll meet another man at the home.

RENA: It's called an adult residence. I don't want to meet another man. One was enough. I always thought Richard was inadequate. I just never had the guts to really leave him. It's no great crime to choose security over passion. My grand passion was the two of you. (*To* BEN.) You have the wonderful wife and the wonderful marriage and have given me my wonderful grandchildren. (*To* NED.) You have the artistic talent, which you inherited from me. Hurry up and write whatever it is you're going to write about me so I can get through all the pain it'll no doubt cause me.

NED: Why do you automatically assume it will be painful?

RENA: Knowing you it will be. I want to show you something. (*Goes into her bedroom.*)

BEN: We can't die. We're indestructible. We have her genes inside us. Sara called. Timmy has to have an operation. But then it should be fine. His bleeding will stop. Finally. All these years we blamed ourselves. It wasn't bad parenting. It wasn't psychosomatic. It was genetic. Ulcerated nerve ends, not dissimilar to what Richard must have had.

NED: I'm glad. Genetic. That's what they say now about homosexuality. In a few more minutes the Religious Right is going to turn violently Pro-Choice.

BEN: Now if Betsy wouldn't keep falling for all these wretched young men who treat her so terribly.

NED: Yes, that's a tough one.

BEN: But I've found her the best therapist I could find.

NED: Her very own first therapist.

BEN: We learned how to attack problems and not be defeated by them. We found the tools to do this, probably by luck and the accident of history. Rena and Richard didn't. For them it was more about missed opportunities. It was the wrong time for them and it hasn't been for us.

NED: For you.

BEN: Ned, you're not going to die. Tell Rena I'll be here with the car in the morning at nine sharp.

(RENA *comes back dressed in the Russian peasant clothing.*)

NED: How *did* we get out of here alive?

BEN: A lot of expensive therapy. (*Sneaks out.*)

RENA: I wore this when I got off the boat from Russia.

NED: You were two years old when you got off the boat from Russia. (*Pause.*) I wore it, too.

RENA: You never wore this.

NED: Daddy beat me up for it.

RENA: Oh, he did not. He never laid a finger on you. How can you say such an awful thing? How about giving us one tiny little bit of credit while I'm still alive.

NED: Mom . . . aren't you afraid of dying?

(HANNIMAN *comes in to take a sample of* NED'S *blood.*)

RENA: Of course I'm frightened. Who isn't? What time is it? My friends are throwing me a farewell party. I see your brother left without saying good-bye. It's as if he's punishing me. He thinks I never notice. You think I don't know how you both treat me with such disdain? So many of my friends have kids who never see them at all. So I guess I must consider myself fortunate. You'll never guess what happened. I called Drew Keenlymore! He's listed in Vancouver. His very first words to me were, "My dear, I called every Weeks in the New York directory trying to find you." He tried to find me. He tried to find me. (*Re:* HANNIMAN.) What is she doing?

NED: A blood test.

RENA: Is my son going to be all right?

NED: My mother, Mrs. Weeks. Nurse Hanniman.

HANNIMAN: What a kind, pleasant, thoughtful, considerate son you have. I'm so enjoying taking care of him.

NED: Nurse Hanniman and I enjoy a rare bonding.

(HANNIMAN *leaves.*)

Momma . . . you may outlive me.

RENA: Don't say that. My momma was ninety-five years old when she died. She was withered beyond recognition. She was in a crib, mewling, wetting her pants, not knowing anyone, and me trying not to vomit from the putrid smell of urine and her runny stools. She simply would not let go. This old people's home had taken her every last cent for this tiny crib, for no nurse to come and wipe her. I wiped her. I came every day. I sat beside her. She didn't know who I was. My own mother. I'll bet you won't do all that for me. People stick articles under my door. "Your son's sick with that queer disease." "I saw your pervert son on TV saying homosexuals are the same as everyone else." Then, in our current events class we had a report on all the progress that's been made and how much your activists had to do with it and all the women came over and congratulated me. I don't know why, after ninety years, I'm surprised by anything.

NED: There hasn't been any progress.

RENA: Of course there has. Alexander . . .

NED: Yes, Momma?

RENA: He's dead. Drew Keenlymore is dead. I planned a trip to British Columbia, to Banff and Lake Louise, and I called to let him know I was going to be in the vicinity and he's gone and died. I guess we couldn't expect him to wait around for me forever, could we?

NED: No, Momma. I'm sorry.

RENA: Good-bye, darling. It's a long trip back. And I'm having trouble with my tooth. Every time I say good-bye I'm never sure I'm going to see you again. Give me a kiss.

(*They kiss.* NED *hugs her as best he can with his arms connected to the tubing.*)

NED: (*As she begins to leave.*) I wouldn't be a writer if you guys hadn't done what you did.

RENA: Is that something else I'm meant to feel guilty for?

NED: I love being a writer.

RENA: At last.

(RENA *walks off, slowly, holding on to things. She is almost blind.*

HANNIMAN *enters, with* DR. DELLA VIDA, *no longer in official uniform, and takes another blood test.*)

NED: Another one? Why am I having another one so quickly? What happened at the White house? What did *he* say?

TONY: They're cutting our budget.

NED: Your buddy. Is it too pushy of me to inquire as to my and/or your progress?

TONY: We have a fifty-fifty chance.

NED: That's your idea of progress?

TONY: You're not only pushy, you're ... how do your people say it—a kvetch? Just imagine this is the cure and you're the first person getting it.

NED: Can I also imagine the Republicans never being reelected?

HANNIMAN: He'd never work again.

TONY: Oh, I'll find a way. (*Leaves.*)

NED: Did the mouth of Weeks cause a little friction in the house of Della Vida?

HANNIMAN: Congratulations. You're my last patient.

NED: Where are you going?

HANNIMAN: To raise my baby. And be a pushy kvetch wife.

NED: How come?

HANNIMAN: It's somebody else's turn now. I think you can identify with that.

NED: Good luck.

HANNIMAN: You, too. Sweet dreams.

(*She turns out the lights and leaves.*

Darkness. NED *is tossing and turning.*)

NED: (*Screaming out.*) Ben!

BEN: (*Lying on a cot next to him.*) I'm here, Ned.

NED: Ben?

BEN: Yes, Ned.

NED: I'm scared.

BEN: It's all right. Go to sleep.

NED: Ben, I love you.

BEN: I love you, too.

NED: I can't say it enough. It's funny, but life is very precious now.

BEN: Why's it funny? I understand, and it is for me, too. A colleague of mine with terminal cancer went into his bathroom last week and blew his brains out with a shotgun.

(*Dawn is breaking outside.* BEN *gets up. He throws some cold water on his face at the sink.*)

NED: Hey, cheer me up, Lemon.

BEN: They haven't struck us out yet.

NED: What if this doesn't work?

BEN: It's going to work. (*Sits beside him on bed.*)

NED: Even if it does, it will only work for a while.

BEN: Then we'll worry about it in a while.

NED: You've certainly spent a great deal of your life trying to keep me alive, and I've been so much trouble, always trying to kill myself, asking your advice on every breath I take, putting you to the test endlessly.

BEN: I beat you up once.

NED: You beat me up? When?

BEN: We were kids. I was trying to teach you how to tackle in football. You were fast, quick. I thought you could be a quarterback. And you wouldn't do it right. You didn't want to learn. It was just perversity on your part. So I decided to teach you a lesson. I blocked you and blocked you, as hard as I could, much harder than I had to. And then I tackled you, and you'd get up and I'd tackle you again, harder. You just kept getting up for more. I beat you up real bad.

NED: I don't remember any of that. Now why did you go and do all that?

BEN: A thousand reasons and who knows?

NED: I don't want to he cremated. I want to be buried, with a tombstone, so people can come and find me and visit. Do you want to be buried or cremated?

BEN: Neither.

NED: What will they do with you?

BEN: I don't care.

NED: How can you not care?

BEN: I won't be here.

NED: You don't want people to remember you?

BEN: I've never thought about it.

NED: It seems like I've spent my whole life thinking about it. How can you never have thought about it?

BEN: I never thought about it.

NED: Well, think about it.

BEN: I don't want to think about it.

NED: I just thought we could be buried side by side.

BEN: Please, Ned. You're not go—

NED: I've picked out the cemetery. It's a pretty place. George Balanchine is buried there. I danced around his grave. When no one could see me.

BEN: Are we finished with the morbid part of this conversation?

NED: No. I want my name on something. A building. At Yale, for gay students, or in New York. Will you look after that for me?

BEN: You'll have many years to arrange all that yourself.

NED: But you're my lawyer!

BEN: Everything will be taken care of.

NED: Then, the rest of my money, you give to the kids and Sara, please give something special to Sara. You married her and you didn't even love her. And you grew to love her. I'm sorry I never really had that. For very long.

BEN: I want you to know . . . I want you to know . . . I'm proud you've stood up for what you've believed in. I've even been a little jealous of all the attention you've received. I think to myself that if I'd gone off on my own instead of built the firm, I could have taken up some cause and done it better than you. But I didn't do that and you have and I admire you for that.

NED: I guess you could have lived without me. I never could have lived without you. Go back to your hotel.

BEN: I'll see you tomorrow.

(*Lights up.* DR. DELLA VIDA *enters, carrying a long computer print-out. He turns off the computer and then the Ex-Cell-Aerator.*)

NED: The results are in. May I have the winning envelope, please?

TONY: I don't know how much more we can take. Your hoodlums infiltrated my hospital. They destroyed my entire laboratory. (*Throwing him the printout.*)

NED: I guess they want you to admit you don't know what the fuck's going on and go back to the drawing board. I'm worse? I'm worse!

TONY: Yes.

NED: What are you going to do?

TONY: There's nothing I can do.

NED: What do you mean there's nothing you can do? You gave me the fucking stuff! You must have considered such a possibility! You must have some emergency measures!

TONY: Oh, shut up! I am sick to death of you, your mouth, your offspring! You think changing Presidents will change anything? Will make any difference? The system will always he here. The system doesn't change. No matter who's President. It doesn't make any difference who's President! You're scared of dying? Let me tell you the facts of life: it isn't easy to die: you don't die until you have tubes in every single possible opening and orifice and vent and passage and outlet and hole and slit in your ungrateful body. Why, it can take years and years to die. It's much worse than you can even imagine. You haven't suffered nearly enough. (*Leaves.*)

NED: (*Pulls the tubes from his arms. Blood spurts out. Gets out of bed.*) What do you do when you're dying from a disease you need not be dying from? What do you do when the only system set up to save you is a pile of shit run by idiots and quacks? (*Yanks the tubes violently out of the wall apparatus, causing blood to gush out. Then pulls out the six bags of blood, smashing them, one by one, against the walls and floor, to punctuate the next speech.*)

My straight friends ask me over and over and over again: why is it so hard for you to find love? Ah, that is the question, answered, I hope, for you tonight. Why do I never stop believing this fucking plague can he cured!

ALEXANDER: (*Appearing in the bath towels he was first seen in.*) What's going to happen to me?

NED: You're going to go to eleven shrinks. You won't fall in love for forty years. And when a nice man finally comes along and tries to teach you to love him and love yourself, he dies from a plague. Which is waiting to kill you, too.

ALEXANDER: I'm sorry I asked. Do I learn anything?

NED: Does it make any sense, a life? (*Singing*.) "Only make believe I love you . . ."

ALEXANDER: (*Singing*.) "Only make believe that you love me . . ."

NED: When Felix was offered the morphine drip for the first time in the hospital, I asked him, "Do you want it now or later?" Felix somehow found the strength to answer back, "I want to stay a little longer."

NED and ALEXANDER: "Might as well make believe I love you . . ."

NED: "For to tell the truth . . ."

NED and ALEXANDER: "I do."

NED: I want to stay a little longer.

THE END

Credits

Larry Kramer was the co-founder of Gay Men's Health Crisis and the founder of ACT UP. He is the author of *The Normal Heart*, which was selected as one of the 100 Greatest Plays of the Twentieth Century by the Royal National Theatre of Great Britain and is the longest-running play in the history of the New York Shakespeare Festival's Public Theater. He is also the author of *The Destiny of Me*, which was a finalist for the Pulitzer Prize and won an Obie and the Lucille Lortel Award for Best Play. Kramer's screenplay adaptation of D. H. Lawrence's *Women in Love*, a film he also produced, was nominated for an Academy Award. He is a recipient of the Award in Literature from the American Academy of Arts and Letters and was the first creative artist and the first openly gay person to be honored by a Public Service Award from Common Cause. His other plays include *Just Say No* and *Sissies' Scrapbook*. He is currently at work on a new novel, *The American People*.